Mystic Insights

Knowing the Unknown

Dr. Paul Leon Masters

Founder

University of Metaphysics
University of Sedona
International Metaphysical Ministry

Mystical Insights

University of Sedona Publishing
2675 W. State Route 89A, Suite 465
Sedona, Arizona 86336
www.universityofsedona.com

Library of Congress Control Number: 2016939000
Masters, Paul Leon.
Mystical Insights
/ Paul Leon Masters. - 1st ed.
ISBN 978-0-9964596-7-9
1.   Spirituality.   2.   Mind and Body. 3.   Metaphysics.

Disclaimer

The content of this book is not intended to replace any form of professionally licensed care, be it medical, psychological, or any other licensed health modality. The views and ideas expressed, whether in totality or as an adjunct to one's spiritual or religious beliefs, are for use in one's spiritual life. Nothing in the content of this book should be considered as infallible, as life is an ongoing process of awakening to truths and practices known only to God.

PRINTED IN THE UNITED STATES OF AMERICA

Dr. Paul Leon Masters, Founder
January 1935—January 2016

University of Metaphysics
University of Sedona
International Metaphysical Ministry

Paul Leon Masters peacefully made his transition on Sunday, January 10, 2016. His last few days were filled with thoughts and words of love for his students and staff, and he passed gently in his sleep.

Acknowledgements

As my professional work has spanned over so many years there are more than just those customary few that I am grateful to. Each has contributed to my life to make my work possible for so many.

Certainly, I wish to thank my parents, Isabel and Leon, whose combined energies made this life's incarnation possible and whose love of me, human dignity, and perseverance were in alignment with my soul and its purpose.

I acknowledge the following persons who were instrumental in helping to make my work possible. Each was very important in his or her own unique way. The names are not in order of importance but as they came to me in moments of reflected memories:

James McCall - Peggy Dlouhy - Tod Barnes - Penny Anne Frank - Lavone Nicoloff - Helen Fox - Genevieve Horton - Linda Gray – Michelle Angela Behr - Ronald Wilson - Sandra Smith Masters

While my soul entered this life with accumulated awareness gathered over many lifetimes, a special thanks to my professor Minor C. Hutchison, with whom I studied metaphysical philosophy for several years, and whose teachings brought to light previous knowledge of mystically founded psychology, philosophy, and spirituality. Also, I will always have so much gratitude to the soul of Swami Vivekananda—wherever in this universe you may be. Although we never met on this physical Earth plane, your teachings complemented and vastly enlarged what I had been reawakened to though this life's metaphysical studies.

Of course, I give a very special thanks to all my students through the years whose support, both financial and spiritual, allowed my research and teachings to cross the half-century mark.

Above all else, I thank Universal Mind/Spirit by whose Grace and Will anything accomplished was made possible. My soul is humbly grateful that I have been used as an instrument of your Presence.

Table of Contents

Preface

As I write this, I am in my 56th year of full-time professional work involving the research and application of research findings to improving human lives. Now in my eighties, my soul's fulfillment continues to be sharing how Universal Mystical Presence and psychic/mystical energy factors influence every aspect of our lives.

Based on research and time-tested applications, what guidance can be shared in the pages of this collection of essays is based on over five decades of full-time research conducted with thousands of my students concerning the nature and reality of consciousness. This was accomplished by taking students into higher states of consciousness while utilizing advanced practices of meditation. Experiences of the students in higher states of meditation were described in research forms. The experiences were studied so that the observations each student gave to his or her experiences could be compared. If both experiences and interpretations were similar, and if such similarities and interpretations were continually produced by large numbers of students, then the experiences became a known truth, reality, or quality for purposes of teaching about the spiritual/psychic/mystical activities of the unconscious.

Such truths were then applied to a spiritual philosophy, psychology, and theology upon which to live daily life. Over a period of years that stretched into decades, these applied truths improved so many students' lives that I chose them to explore in the topics in this book. As such, each essay in this book is a composite or synthesis of what is described as the transcendent, the transpersonal, the psychical, and the mystical or Universal Consciousness or God.

Not a Coincidence

You have this book in your hands because you are ready for its contents. Nothing in this Universe is by chance or coincidence. If you are a long-time student or practitioner of this book's content there will be things with which you are already familiar. The purpose of this book is to expand your knowledge with ideas, concepts, and practices that are new to you.

My Gift to You

Many times over the years, I have been told by students that I have the knack or ability to blend or synthesize so many studies into one cohesive and, above all, applicable approach to improving life through a complementing synthesis of psychical energy factors, namely, the transcendent, the transpersonal, the meditative, and the mystical. Such subjects are most often studied independently of each other without bringing them all together in an intelligible manner so as to make common, practical sense in meeting the needs of the individual and society collectively. May this be so accomplished as you read this book. And, as I was so gifted by Universal Presence—may you be so gifted.

In Service to God's Presence within You,
Paul Leon Masters
March 2015

 *Introduction*

Dr. Masters dedicated over five decades of full-time professional work involving the research and application of research findings to improving human lives. His soul's fulfillment was to share how Universal Mystical Presence and psychic/mystical energy factors influence every aspect of our lives.

The content of this book consists of Mystical Insights realized and explored by him over the course of half a century. Anyone having any interest in reading Mystical Insights is at least on the outer perimeters of consciousness exploration, for the curiosity does not come from personal ego inquisitiveness, but from the stirrings of the soul. These stirrings originate from the Originator of the soul—Universal Consciousness or God.

Dr. Masters was in total agreement with Socrates' observation, "The unexamined life is not worth living." Dr. Masters added to this thought, however, explaining that it could be said that all life is worth living, because eventually, whether in this lifetime or another, life itself will finally bring about self-examination. That examination must be real and complete to go beyond the appearances of five-sense perception or beyond the basis of empirical, scientific evidence of such perception, for only in the unconscious of a human being and other forms of life can Life reveal Itself and

Its mysteries. Upon such revelation alone could one have a realistic perspective on life—and more specifically—on one's own life, prompting such questions as:

- Is there a life after death?
- If there is life after death, what kind of life?
- Do souls reincarnate? If so, why, where, when?
- What are the underpinnings of health and healing?
- What effects do the experiences of higher perception have on a person's life, and are they life altering?
- What is the potential of consciousness in human or other expressions of life?
- What is the soul's purpose in this physical lifetime and beyond?
- How and why did life come to be?
- Above all, is there a Universal Consciousness in Whose Consciousness we move, live, and have our being?

The Eternal Perspective of Universal Consciousness alone (where all that is, has been, and will be) has the answers to life's mysteries—and, most importantly for every single person, the answers as to how and why. All of this truth exists in the unconscious of every person, though all but a very few would even begin to suspect it's there—and even those few tend to view it philosophically. Fewer still have probed it to the fullest.

The same awesome Power of Mind and Spirit that created the Galaxies and gave wisdom to human thought so that it might create in science, the arts, and all human achievement, is the Same Power in you, right this moment, waiting for you to acknowledge its Supreme Presence.

~ Dr. Paul Leon Masters

Real Magic Versus Ego Illusionary Magic

Can people really materialize their needs through spiritual practices? So very many people over the past 100 years have been attracted to metaphysical New Thought by the lure of what they personally can acquire. Certainly there are human needs of a roof overhead, food on the table, clothes on one's back, and other basic necessities. It is then certainly understandable that a person would be attracted to a philosophical theology that offers promise or hope that a person can meet his or her basic needs, and yes, be a prosperous person materially. And, all this is in direct contrast to more fundamentalist religion that has either directly or indirectly suggested to followers that being prosperous is somehow sinful or not being religious.

Over many decades it was my God-bestowed privilege to speak before many metaphysically-oriented audiences. I did so often experience sadness as I did, because the vast majority of those who had practiced Metaphysical New Thought had not, in metaphysical New Thought vocabulary, demonstrated or materialized what they had hoped. Yes, they had prayed, affirmed, thought positively, meditated, and engaged perhaps in a vast array of other metaphysical practices—and yet—there was not anything even near to what they had been seeking; and when I say they, I mean what their personal egos said they should have. In such a state of personal ego consciousness, the best that can be achieved, which is what most metaphysical New Thought followers acquire, is to feel a little more positive about their lives and live in the hope that somehow their metaphysical practices will finally bring them great materializations or demonstrations.

And herein lies spiritual quicksand. For to let one's mind get so caught up in getting so as to satisfy what the personal ego believes it needs and in many cases has been led to believe it needs is to have a whole life through the influence of others. To the point—the personal ego or illusionary identity does not really know what reality, Universal Consciousness, or God knows— which is what is best for one's soul self. To then practice any of the teachings of metaphysical New Thought without first setting aside the personal ego's illusionary needs and wants and replacing them with real identification with God's inner Presence is an exercise in futility.

The Christ Mind that was in Jesus expressed it this way, "Seek first the kingdom of heaven [contact with Universal or God Consciousness] within you—and all things will be added unto you." By way of practical example, let's say a person has a new smart television able to hook up to the Internet and produce 3D images. Now a person can stand in front of this device and pray to it, affirm to it, meditate on it, think positively about it, but none of its features—no picture, no sound, no Internet—will be activated, demonstrated, or

2

materialized unless—it is plugged into the wall!

Real Magic alone is the Power and Will which created life and sustains it and which alone can materialize anything and everything in a human's life. What this means is that praying, affirming, meditating, visualizing can only be productive if the personal ego and its will are set aside and the will of the Universe and God are given absolute control over one's life. God's Universe will then intuitively lead and guide one as to what is really best for the soul within oneself. All the praying, visualizing, meditating then are not causing God to improve one's life—rather, being in a state of cooperative consciousness with the Universe or God brings about improvements in one's life according to Universal Will or God's Will.

Advice?

Downgrade the false personal ego identity to the nothingness that it really is. Upgrade your identity to reality by entering into cooperative consciousness with God's Presence and Will for life's experience—on this physical plane of existence and beyond it through eternity.

For further clarification, prayer, visualization, and affirmations are effective if your conscious awareness is connected to the Universal God Consciousness within you.

When this Mystical Connection is present, prayer

becomes Universal Consciousness thinking through you. Prayer becomes God's thoughts in self-contemplation, which are attuning your body, mind, and soul to be in harmony with what is best for you. Visualizations are God's pictorial images being placed in your consciousness—again, for the purpose of attuning your body, mind, and soul to be in harmony with what is best for you.

When you affirm, it is God and God's thoughts you are affirming for your body, mind, and soul. It is good to point out again that without mystical connection, the false personal ego identity is in charge of one's affirmations. The Christ Mind that was in Jesus spoke of this in the words, "for all their vain [personal ego] repetitions [affirming], they will not be heard."

Prayer, visualizations, and affirmations are effective when no longer practiced by one's false personal ego but under the control of God's Universal Consciousness within oneself. Real magic is to be found in the words, "not my will [false, personal ego sense of identity]—but Thy Will [Universal God's Will] be done."

Thankfulness in Mystical Reality

Everything that exists physically—even ideas thought by those in physical embodiment—has a deeper, more profound energy existence. The idea of thanks is part of a deeper, more mystical reality as well. A person who expresses thanks for any physical life experience is not, in the majority of cases, aware of the profoundness of his or her expression. A person expressing thanks to God may have little if any awareness of the deeper significance of such an expression. This is so because, unless a person has been blessed with real mystical awareness, giving thanks is an expression of limited, personal ego identity.

It may be that when giving thanks to God, there can be a divide of consciousness or awareness between personal ego identity and universal identity or God. Because of such a divide imagined by the personal ego, the full mystical reality of the idea of is lost in the myriad of personal ego subterfuges. When the personal ego gives thanks to God, the ego is one thing or identity and God is another identity.

In contrast, when a person with real mystical awareness gives thanks to God, there is a knowingness that there is but one life in this Universe, and that one life or Universal Consciousness is God. In absolute mystical reality, when giving thanks is expressed, it is God's Presence thanking God's Presence—God's Presence acknowledging Itself for the good, excellence, and creativity achieved in human embodiment or, to use the Biblical expression, "The Spirit made flesh."

In mystical reality, the most important thing a person should be aware of is that giving thanks acknowledges God's Presence, if thanks are given to God. The more one gives thanks to God, the more one's consciousness is filled with the Presence of God, which increases mystical union, whether in or out of meditation or any other spiritual practice.

Sometimes, persons with an awareness of mystical reality thank another person and are aware that they are not thanking another person's personal ego, but rather, the God Presence within the other person which stimulated the person's soul to do something that prompted the expression of thanks. In absolute mystical reality, giving thanks is God's Presence speaking to Itself within Itself, or what might be called universal self-contemplation.

The concept of time also enters into the mystical reality of thanks. When a person traditionally gives thanks, it is for something in the physical time zone of reference that has already happened and, in fewer cases, is concurrently happening, and in fewer still, for anything to be happening in the future. In absolute mystical reality, all three physical time references are present in the expression of thanks—for the past, for the present, and for the future.

People with genuine mystical awareness would find themselves saying at least once daily, "I give thanks to God's Presence for all blessings received in the past, the present, and the future." Even a person who has not achieved mystical awareness but recognizes the validity of such a statement on a philosophical level could use such an affirmation of the mystical reality of thanks.

Those living in mystical reality exist in one eternal moment of time, when past, present, and future co-exist. In such a reality the future has already happened. When people then give thanks for blessings or good in the future, they are acknowledging good that they have already received but have yet to be made aware of in their sense perception.

The mystical bottom line: whenever people give thanks, they are in mystical reality interfacing with God's Presence.

What can be learned from all this? Give thanks to God often—very often.

Loneliness—
Mystically Perceived

From a king sitting in a palace to a head of a government, loneliness can be an ever-present state of consciousness. Like those who rule, loneliness is also present in the lives of those whom one might not suspect of feeling such loneliness: people who are married or in a significant relationship may also feel loneliness; those whose lives are surrounded by many people through family or social ties as well as business or career ties may also feel the presence of loneliness. Perhaps only those who consider themselves loners seem immune to loneliness—yet even they will experience periods or cycles of loneliness.

It could certainly be said then that all situations that would seem to be barriers to loneliness are ineffectual to its presence—be it power, fame, fortune, or other manners of worldly cures against feeling that one is isolated or disconnected from even those who would seem closest.

In today's modern world, the advancement of science increases for many the feeling of loneliness, as the vastness of both outer and inner space, viewed strictly from a physical perspective, diminishes the illusionary identity of personal ego existence. The enormity of outer space and the complexities of inner space, as postulated in recent times by quantum physics, fuel an even greater feeling of insecurity by the false, personal ego identity as it scrambles to find or secure its relationship to a world that is only perceived by the five senses.

And herein lies the truth of why loneliness is so widespread—the absence of relationship. People can only feel loneliness when they feel that they have no real relationships in their lives. Some try to bridge this feeling of not having a relationship with people by finding or living for some cause, be it humanitarian, spiritual, or, to another extreme, on some battlefield. At best, however, this is covering up the symptoms temporarily and not really finding a cure for the presence of loneliness.

When a person feels loneliness, what they are really feeling is the isolation experienced by the false, imaginary sense of personal ego identity. They do not feel or experience any real sense of union or oneness with other false, personal ego identities. How could they? What you have is one falsehood, or false identity, trying to have an experience of oneness with another falsehood. Two wrongs don't make a right—or two illusions do not a reality make. Without reality there is no foundation to any relationship. Is it any wonder then that there is such widespread loneliness in this physical, Earth plane of existence?

The answer to emerging from loneliness is to emerge from the illusion that one's sense of personal ego identity is who or what a person really is. Forming a relationship between the true, universal soul identity within oneself and God (the Universal Soul identity, or Universal Spirit) transmutes isolation from others and the Universe to oneness, allness, and a relationship to the wholeness that is life.

This becomes the spiritual alchemist's achievement of turning base metal (the personal ego identity) into gold—Universal Consciousness identity. There is an old Hindu expression, which goes, "It is not for the sake of my beloved—but rather for the sake of God's Presence within my beloved that I love him."

Loneliness, mystically understood then, is isolation from God and from the Presence of God within others. Extending this further into what some have called extroverted mysticism, it becomes isolation from nature or what might be called poetically, God's Face—isolation from sensing God's Presence in the trees, the flowers, the birds, and so on. Absolute oneness is the absolute relationship. In such oneness there is no isolation or apartness. Identity is not so concerned about being loved as it is with loving.

Can such an ideal solving of loneliness be achieved? Yes, it can. Can it be lasting throughout one's life? Because outer sense impressions can be so illusionary, there can be certain periods when the old, false, personal ego might try to re-establish itself. But these are brief periods. In the earlier mistranslations of Jesus' Aramaic language, it sounds as though Jesus experienced this brief lapse on the cross with the words, "My God, My Father, why has Thou forsaken me?" But the accurate translation of Jesus' words from the cross shows that Jesus truly spoke in his Universal Soul identity with his words, "My God, My God, how has Thou glorified me!" *Eli, Eli, lama sabachthan!*

Advice?

People who feel loneliness should daily, if not many times daily, renounce their false, personal ego identities and proclaim their universal soul identity, Christ Mind Consciousness (or by whatever name one chooses to call it) and give it up to the oneness of all, God's Presence and Will. In so doing, they achieve a connection or relationship with all that really is and an understanding of that which only appears to be.

Or, in the words of the Christ Mind that was in Jesus, "I am in this world, but not of it."

Participate in this world of illusions but always retain the light of universal awareness, wherever your soul's purpose path may lead you.

Be connected—very connected.

Exploring Consciousness

Introduction to Findings

I was initially inspired to study and explore consciousness as a result of experiencing various forms of Eastern meditation in my youth. As consciousness opened before my inner sight and revealed existence beyond my sense perception, the curiosity mounted within me: Would the same revelations that I was experiencing be experienced by others? If so, would the explanations of what they experienced be the same as mine? I knew the effect that such disclosure of unconscious truth was having on my psyche—but what about the impact on others?

Such questions led me to open the Institute of Parapsychology in 1959, located in Beverly Hills, California, which is where a of forty-year journey of consciousness exploration began. The aim of the Institute was to research higher and expanded states of consciousness as they related to spiritual reality and human self-betterment. This goal was accomplished through Eastern forms of advanced meditation together with adaptable forms of self-hypnotic techniques. Thousands of research experiences by experimenting students were recorded, and the effects on their practical daily lives and spiritual unfoldment were noted and studied. Also during this time, numerous meditation students came forward to be trained as teachers.

The findings of such explorations evolved into the teachings and curriculum of the University of Metaphysics, the University of Sedona, and the psychology, philosophy, and theology of the International Metaphysical Ministry.

This Mystical Insight comes as a result of those four decades of consciousness exploration with thousands of students and teachers.

Findings

The exploration of consciousness is the final frontier in the exploration of life and the mysteries of existence—its origin, its on-going presence—as well as for answering questions that intellectual analysis cannot answer because it is based on the speculations of the five senses.

Indeed, to find the truths of life, a person must go beyond the limitations of the five senses. The outer senses can only perceive on a limited scale. Even with the help of scientific instruments piercing minute information through the lenses of a microscope or exploring the vastness of outer space with a telescope or an exploratory landing craft, there remains a limitation to some answers.

Did the Universe originate by chance? Is a person simply a matter of some cosmic coincidence? Nothing in the scientific arsenal of five-sense, empirical evidence can form any conclusions without entering the province of speculation. The eternal perspective of Universal Consciousness alone (where all that is, has been, and will be exists) has the answers to life's mysteries—and, most importantly for every single person, the answers as to how and why. All of this truth exists in the unconscious of every person, though all but a very few would even begin to suspect it's there—and even those few tend to view it philosophically. Fewer still have probed it to the fullest.

Socrates observed, "The unexamined life is not worth living." Considering this thought further, however, it could be said that all life is worth living, because eventually, whether in this lifetime or another, life itself will finally bring about self-examination. That examination must be real and complete to go beyond the appearances of five-sense perception or beyond the basis of empirical, scientific evidence of such perception, for only in the unconscious of a human being and other forms of life can life reveal itself and its mysteries. Upon such revelation alone can one have a realistic perspective on life, and more specifically, on one's own life, prompting such questions as:

- Is there a life after death?
- If there is life after death, what kind of life?
- Do souls reincarnate? If so, why, where, when?

- What are the underpinnings of health and healing?
- What effects do the experiences of higher perception have on a person's life, and are they life altering?
- What is the potential of consciousness in human or other expressions of life?
- What is the soul's purpose in this physical lifetime and beyond?
- How and why did life come to be?
- Above all, is there a Universal Consciousness—God—in whose consciousness, "We move, live, and have our being?"

Only through the exploration of the consciousness hidden in the unconscious can such questions be answered. We live in eternity, and there is so-called time enough for every soul to begin to question and enter into extensive self-examination and explore inner consciousness.

There are those who are ready for such exploration—and those few in number, in comparison to the world's population, are still a sufficient number to have a spiritual awakening, whether channeled through the arts, commerce, science, leadership, athletics, or religion.

Anyone having any interest in reading *Mystical Insights* is at least on the outer perimeters of consciousness exploration, for the curiosity does not come from personal ego inquisitiveness but from the stirrings of the soul. These stirrings originate from the originator of the soul—Universal Consciousness or God. Follow your spiritual heartbeat, for it is Universal Consciousness or God calling you to know and to be one with the eternal.

Written with love to the few who are ready to explore and to all who will be.

A Universally Conscious Mind

St. Paul once proclaimed "Let this Mind be in you, which was also in Christ Jesus."

Richard Maurice Bucke had this experience and, in his now classic book titled *Cosmic Consciousness*, he writes about some of the many people he believed had also experienced cosmic or Universal Consciousness through the ages.

In recent years, through advancement in communications, there has been a surge of both hard copy and eBooks speaking on the subject, but most who speak or write on the subject are commentators or observers that have not themselves had such an awakening.

The descriptions given in this Mystical Insight come as a direct result of over half a century of numerous experiences of Universal Consciousness. These experiences place me above no one, for Universal Consciousness simply is and has existed in the experience of many persons through the ages. To what extent Universal Consciousness has dominated the consciousness of any single individual can be a great variable.

The experiences of awareness described below are offered only for points of reference from the standpoint of earthly perception when speaking of a Universal Consciousness of being:

- An identification with the whole of existence
- A oneness with the whole of existence
- A recognition that the level of spiritual awareness at the surface level of most human minds is at great variance and that the vast majority of souls incarnating on the physical Earth plane have little if any awareness of their universal origin and inseparable oneness with Universal Consciousness. This is not a criticism, but rather an observation that the majority of souls incarnating here are more in the embryonic stage of spiritual awakening.
- A recognition and awareness that the physical Earth plane is an existence into which souls of a lesser degree of spiritual awareness incarnate
- A recognition that, because of the enormous variety of spiritual awakening, various religions exist to be able to communicate spirituality to those on the same level
- An awareness that life is Universal and not confined to one physical, Earth plane incarnation—that the real life in each soul is universal life or eternal life and cannot die or cease to exist when the present human body is no longer available
- A forgiveness and compassion for all souls, recognizing their lack of awareness of the

oneness of life—but while forgiving and compassionate, not condoning any act that violates the sacred oneness of life. Note these words from the Universal Consciousness, the Christ Mind that was in Jesus:

"Forgive them, Father, for they know not what they do."
"Who among you is without sin and will cast the first stone?"
"Sin no more."

- A recognition that Universal Consciousness or mind existed in the Mind of Jesus as well as in Buddha, Krishna, Mohammed, and many others. Its manifestation expressed itself at an exceptional level in the Christ Mind in Jesus—that is, the forgiveness of sins and negative, destructive karma for all souls incarnating into this plane of existence. The message for all those who believe in the Christ (Universal, eternal life) that was in Jesus is that they "shall be forgiven and live an eternal life." This same Universal Consciousness of forgiveness can also be found in the words of others. Krishna, as an example, said "Though a man be filled with the sins of a lifetime, if he but love me (Universal God Consciousness) in complete adoration, I see no sinner, as that man is holy."
- An awareness of other dimensions of existence and the progressive awakening of souls to higher levels of manifestation. And, when the reference

is made to souls awakening to Universal Consciousness on the physical Earth plane, in higher or more advanced souls it is more a re-awakening to Universal Consciousness, which generally occurs earlier in such a person's life as consciousness expands beyond simple ego-centered existence.

- An awareness that true and thus lasting wealth is to be found in oneness with Universal Consciousness or God. In the words of the Christ Mind that was in Jesus, "Your treasure is where your heart is." Ego-centered minds will often challenge those who have spoken about or alluded to oneness with God with the criticism that if one is so aligned with oneness, shouldn't one have the power to create power, fame, fortune, and so on? In the words of the Christ Mind that was in Jesus, "My kingdom is not of this world." In Universal Consciousness there is so much more—so very, very much more, that the trinkets of this world are seen for what they are. But if a person of Universal Consciousness has achieved much by worldly standards, there is still no obsession with achievement or identity expansion as measured against worldly standards. All possessions or achievements are recognized as temporary illusions of the outer senses: a better home, car, or financial state are just seen as ways to an end—to be in a better position to do things to glorify God, not the personal ego. A simple flower may be of far greater value to a person having Universal Consciousness than a diamond; but if such a person possesses a diamond or anything of similar earthly value, it is, again, used as a resource to bring Universal Consciousness or God before others, whether in direct spiritual expression or indirectly through art, music, poetry, science, athletics, and leadership, to name but a few.

Universal Mind Consciousness only takes place when the soul is ready to experience it. Even the most advanced meditation techniques and other spiritual practices will not cause such awareness to occur. In a few people such practices will seem to be the cause, but are not. These people are engaged in such practices because there was already a stirring in their souls that an awakening was about to take place.

If you intuitively sense such a stirring in yourself and if your soul's time is in this lifetime, give thanks to universal God Presence within you—for you are blessed!

Two Christianities—
the Known and the Unknown

For over 2,000 years, there have been two Christianities—the exoteric, or generally accepted, one that most people who identify themselves as Christians believe in and the other, the one that the Christ Mind in Jesus taught only to the disciples. The teaching that was taught to the disciples, or the esoteric teaching—was the mystical.

In the infinite wisdom of the Christ Mind or Universal Consciousness was the recognition that the broad masses of people who incarnate on to this physical Earth plane are young souls with limited capacity of spiritual awareness. Such souls can only assimilate what is said or experienced up to a certain level of spiritual awareness. As everyone lives in Eternity, these souls will, through many incarnations, grow in awareness until they awaken to a higher Universal Consciousness of reality and Universal selfhood. Until that time, they have the exoteric or outer Christianity to give them belief in God and the continuance of life beyond the physical.

Until our awareness has awakened to the Universal, we live in more personal, ego-centered awareness. Any other spiritual belief is a challenge to the ego identity, which has accepted the exoteric as being the "final word" or authority on religion and thus on the fragile support system that maintains the personal, ego identity. It is not therefore surprising that when the mass of exoteric Christians encounter anything of the esoteric or mystical teachings of Christ, they cannot identify it as being Christian. Exoteric Christians through the ages have oftentimes labeled mystics as heretics. Their judgment is both understandable and forgivable, as they were without higher universal awareness.

It is also noteworthy that even those souls whose awareness has reawakened beyond fundamentalist, exoteric Christianity to more of a Metaphysical, New Thought awareness may not possess esoteric or mystical awareness, except perhaps on a philosophic or intellectual level. Just as one would think one is now at a higher spiritual plateau of understanding through Metaphysical, New Thought Christianity—so much higher than the fundamentalist—there will one day come the revelation that there is far more awakening, far more to realize about universal spiritual reality and the esoteric, mystical teachings of Christ. You see, with few exceptions, the fundamentalist and the Metaphysical, New Thought person are both functioning basically on a personal, ego-centered level of awareness. Both the fundamentalist and the Metaphysical, New Thought souls may come from a common position, be it concerning physical substance or an afterlife: What can I get from God?

By comparison, the esoteric or mystically aware souls are concentrated on "What can I give to God?" God is the center around which one's life is built by giving up the false sense of personal, ego identity and its will, to be replaced by seeking to do God's Will as intuitively guided to do so.

The esoteric, mystical, or other Christianity that the Christ Mind taught to the disciples is based on direct, firsthand experience of Higher Consciousness. There is very direct reference to this inner, esoteric, mystical experience that He taught the disciples in the following words in the New Testament:

> For verily I say unto you, that many prophets and righteous men have desired to see those things which ye see and have not seen them; and to hearthose things which ye hear and have not heard them. (Matt 13: 17; King James Version)

The Christ Mind that was in Jesus had taught the Christ Mind, Universal Consciousness that was within the disciples how to open to the direct, firsthand experience of higher spiritual realities—to actually see and sometimes hear reality beyond the five senses.

Actually, before the incarnation of Jesus and the disciples, they had all been chosen to live the life they did and be part of the Christ story that was to unfold on the physical Earth plane. Far more so than ever realized, certain pacts or agreements are made between souls before physical incarnation. Such agreements or what might be called "soul contracts" are not confined only to highly spiritual souls, but exist at all levels. Just as Jesus was supposed to meet up with his disciples, so, too, have you have been drawn to souls that you had a common spiritual destiny with before this incarnation.

In the world of the two Christianities, there is neither one that is right nor one that is wrong. Each has its place, because both have been created by God to fulfill the souls of different levels of awareness. The truly wise and mystically aware are aware of this co-existent expression.

The Christ Mind that was in Jesus incarnated to bring two teachings—one that could be understood by the masses and one that could be understood by the few, until those that are the masses today become the few of the future.

Whatever level of Christianity or any other faith that one may be in, ultimately all souls are blessed by having been given life by the One—that is, life itself, Universal God Consciousness.

Peace and good will to the wide variance of souls everywhere.

Looking Back...
Into the Future

As life for every soul unfolds until its conscious Awareness, the surface part of the mind waits in anticipation of what the future will be. Will there be improvements in finances, love, health, happiness? Or will things continue as they have been or—God forbid—will they worsen?

Many decades ago, a song that was popular had lyrics that went, " . . . whatever will be, will be . . . the future's not ours to see, que será, será." The lyrics maintained that what will be—will be, suggesting that one had little power of what will be. This of course flies in the face of the personal human ego, which to justify its existence asserts that it does have the power, in and of itself, to mold or shape the future.

However, mystically speaking, we live in an illusion of time and space—a veritable cosmic house of smoke and mirrors. What to the outer five senses seems to be reality may be but a dim image of what is—or is not. Every time there seems to be a new event in a person's life—be it a new year, new job, new house, new car—on the surface it may seem new, but in mystical reality it is old or even ancient if we give up the illusion of time.

It can be said that when we wonder about the future, we are, in mystical fact, looking back into the past. In piercing into reality, mystical awareness knows that past, present and future are one, as when we yield the illusion of time, it is revealed that there is no separation between past, present, and future.

Many have used the phrase "the future is now," which could be considered in one respect correct—but even more revealing would be the words "the future is past." That may sound like an alarming thought to many because it may subtly suggest that humans cease in their efforts to improve the seeming future. The reality is that human attempts to improve things should go on because they are part of the seeming future (which is already the past). As an example, should one pray if what will be has already happened? It depends on one's level of awareness. If more bound by the personal ego—the answer would be yes. If free of the personal ego's illusions, the prayer might be spoken in such words as "I give thanks to God's Presence—that God's Will has been done." It's saying that however things have already turned out, they are for the best in the eternal long run because they are in accordance with the Will of God for the eternal good of the soul.

Candidly, the more we release our personal will to the will of God, the more we have the realization that the Eternal has total and complete charge and that human efforts to improve are only a playing out of a cosmic script on the stage of eternal life, while the eternal director, or God, knows that the curtain has already come down and all that seeming future is already past.

Things simply cannot be left up to the devices of mortal awareness, because mortal awareness does not have the capacity to see the whole picture. Only Universal Consciousness in self-contemplation can direct life so that there is life—at least as it is humanly perceived. Only the false sense of personal ego identity feels uncomfortable with glimpses of a greater reality. But when the false sense of self is diminished in one's life, there comes a state of increased peace in one's soul. Life goes on, but without the stresses of a personal ego identity placing pressures on the health of the body and the fulfillment of the soul. Life goes on with an awareness that a role is to be played in what already is the history of the past. To do well, to accomplish improvement, is to be an integral part of a wonderful history that already is.

In basic teachings of Metaphysical, New Thought spirituality are the words, "I give thanks that it is already so—and so it is!" Such an affirmation is thought by some to make something so by saying it already is so. But the higher mystical truth is that whatever is affirmed is already past, not because an affirmation has made it so, but because God's Will, knowing the greater good for the soul, made something so.

The Mind of God is not some blank slate where a mortal mind can impose its will without an awareness of the ramifications. Universal Consciousness or the Mind of God is always in charge of its own thoughts, whether they be images of galaxies, other dimensions or inhabitants, or human life forms.

Universal Consciousness or God has already worked out what we call human life in a much greater scheme of things. Every person has already awakened to the full soul's potential—a oneness with God's Presence, God's Expression, God's Will, and in such oneness—God's Love.

This is a future worth looking back into.

Resolving the Unresolvable

To wish, to hope, to dream of better things is a state of mind through which most people look upon every new cycle in their lives. This is especially true at the beginning of humanity's group cycle at the dawn of every New Year.

Hoping and dreaming of making things better in their lives, people make resolutions that they will live or be a certain way, that they will make changes in their lives or how they will go about doing things. Yet, whether these resolutions occur at the time of a new year or at any other time, so very many of them remain unfulfilled or unresolved.

For most people, the story is very much the same. Well-intentioned resolutions seem to fade away and become distant cobwebs in the closet of the mind. Periodically, something then happens that reminds them that what they once resolved—remains unresolved. Why did I not follow through, we ask ourselves, when it was so evident that a change for the better was necessary?

The human dilemma repeats itself time and again: the struggle of the false sense of personal ego identity struggling within itself. From the inner whisper of Spirit comes the guidance, "this is the chance to make things better," only to be responded to by the shouting back of the personal ego, "this is why I can't or won't." There is the Biblical observation, "a house divided against itself cannot stand." This certainty is played out in the inner lives of most people today in the battle between truth, God and falsehood—the false sense of personal ego identity.

In mystical reality, that is—in the Mind of God—all is already resolved in the eternity of beingness. But in the seeming illusion of time, within the false, personal ego identity—things remain unresolved. Now there's a single reason for this: If everything were resolved, everything would be perfect or God Beingness, and the personal ego would cease to be. The very existence of a false sense of personal ego identity is dependent on the seeming dualism of the resolved and unresolved—upon inner conflict. Whenever a person resolves to make changes in life, a dualistic conflict takes place, creating a stalemate where all remains unresolved.

Again, consider the Biblical statement "you can't put new wine into old wineskins." Similarly, you can't put new resolutions into the old bottles of the false, personal ego identity and achieve improved results. If a resolution is to be made, the first should be, "I give up my false sense of personal ego identity and will to the Universal Consciousness of God and God's Will, and in so doing, whatever seems to be in need of being resolved is already resolved in the Mind of God." Consider these Biblical words of great mystical transformation: "He who loses himself [one's false sense of personal ego], finds himself [one's true beingness—a oneness of soul with Universal Consciousness or God]."

The person with true mystical awareness sees the false, personal ego identity as a game player who repeatedly presents the doctrine of the unresolved before the limited perception of the physical senses. In mystical awareness—all is already resolved.

What to do?

Meditate daily, letting go to God's Presence within oneself. In so doing you raise yourself up to a higher vantage point of awareness where you can look down on physical life and see the light that is—rather than the illusionary life-shadows of reality.

Affirm daily—that all that you could ever hope to be resolved is already resolved in the Mind of God, and then trust in God's eternal timetable as to when it will be revealed to you.

Stop praying, affirming, and visualizing what you can get from God and move upward in conscious beingness to realize what you can give to God—your body, mind, and soul. Only then will God begin to show you that all is resolved, and the measure of one's life is God's yardstick alone.

In your true self—be at peace in this eternal moment of always.

Transitional Gender Incarnating

Honoring our differences, so long as they are not self-destructive or bring harm to others, is honoring God, for all differences between people in the final analysis are individualized expressions of God.

Religion through the ages has so very often divided people—labeling some as being on the side of God's Will and others as some lower order of life. This religious influence has brought great misery, for example, to the lives of many whose sexuality was not heterosexual. To the religious extremist, to be gay, lesbian, bi-sexual, or transsexual is to be anti-God. This has led to much prejudice, violence, and even killing of people whose manner of sexual expression and interest is in contrast to heterosexuals.

Mystically, all life is seen and known to be an expression of God individualized into form and embodiment. All that is can only be so because the Ultimate God Power and Will of the Universe has created it to be so, and that includes how every soul comes into physical manifestation. Each human form and manifestation is a God-directed manifestation, not a human-governed choice.

Here's the Reality:

Life is an on-going process. There is nothing motionless in the manifesting of life by Spirit, Universal Consciousness, or God. All that is, is constantly on the move, constantly processing. Life's process is also one of constant refinement to achieve balance within the soul-self—that part of everyone that is closest to Universal Consciousness.

Balance is constantly being gained or lost as the soul-self passes through various stages of spiritual awakening to its ultimate oneness with God. A balancing pendulum swings back and forth through physical lifetimes and non-physical lifetimes (between physical incarnations), a process involving the balancing of masculine and feminine energies at each progressive level of spiritual awakening.

Everything is in motion, including gender expression. If a soul is lacking masculine energy to achieve balance at a certain level of spiritual awakening, the masculine energy force will be automatically increased whether the soul is in physical or non-physical astral embodiment.

As this balancing of male and female energies is constantly a work in progress, a soul whose time has come once again to incarnate physically may be in a transitional part of the process. Thus when this soul enters physical embodiment, the gender is in a state of transitional process—transferring from masculine to feminine or feminine to masculine—possibly with no one energy clearly defined or dominant.

Everyone who may be gay, lesbian, bi-sexual, or transsexual is in the process of a transitional gender change. This gender change is usually gradual over many lifetimes. Every soul goes through it with each level of spiritual awakening so as to achieve ultimate balance, which is ultimate harmony, ultimate peace, ultimate awareness, ultimate oneness, love universal, and God Presence.

It should be noted that even those who express the most heterosexual energies are quietly, within the hidden depths of the unconscious or soul-self, undergoing a transitional process for the sake of balancing—at whatever spiritual level of awakening they are. When, in more everyday conversation we use such phrases as "bringing forth more of one's feminine or masculine side," we are in fact alluding to this balancing process.

When a person has truly awakened to a higher degree of mystical spiritual awareness, all life expressions are seen as one life or God, expressing through human life forms the ongoing process of male and female energy balancing that all gender expressions are processing under the will and power of Universal Consciousness or God. For religions of differing beliefs to suggest to their followers that God considers those living lives in a transitional state of gender process to be wrong, only demonstrates their lack of spiritually awakened awareness.

All that is—is of God, One Universal Life—and because of this the differences between people and between transitional gender expression should be honored as another part of God's Beingness and Will. If God does not will it so, it will not be.

In a world of illusionary, five-sense perceptions much may seem divided or different from oneself. In a world awakened to Universal One Life Consciousness/Spirit that is God, all is whole and at peace, and in that wholeness, the oneness that is God's Love for all its creations is expressed.

The closer you are to God, the further you are from illusions that divide.

Simultaneous Dimensional Existence

We are many in one.

When the psalmist praised God, proclaiming himself "fearfully and wonderfully made" (Psalm 139), he alluded to the mysteries of our beingness that mystics through the ages had discovered—that the reality of who and what we are is complex. Indeed every human being is a microcosm of the macrocosmic Universe, both physical and nonphysical.

How complex is a person's state of beingness? If a person had no idea of the inner physiology of the human body and suddenly viewed it for the first time, most assuredly there would be a sense of amazement. Consider then that there are still other levels to a person's state of beingness that are just as complex, if not far more so.

Every day of human life most people go about their lives not thinking about the physiological workings of their bodies—simply accepting that their outer reflections in their mirrors reflect who they are. Only when people are not feeling well are they reminded that they are more than the outer image of themselves. So barring illness, most people go about their lives without an awareness of the intricacies taking place in the inner workings of their bodies.

Beyond the inner, physiological workings of the physical body, there exists the same lack of awareness about other levels of activity composing one's beingness. What mystics through the ages have discovered is that a person's beingness extends into other dimensions of existence, with a corresponding level of consciousness for each of those existences. In first encounters with such revelations, this can be startling.

As an illustration, most religions tell their followers that when they pass on from this physical world their souls will travel to heaven or some other after-death state. Yet, if the mystical truth be told, everyone already exists in an after-death or astral plane. We exist there all our physical lives, from the time we take our first physical breath—and yes, even before that. This other existence is another dimensional energy body that is a part of one of several dimensions that make up one's beingness.

To add to this mystery of one's beingness—conscious life activity exists at every level of one's beingness. In the case of one's astral or after-death body, an astral life is already being simultaneously lived. Passing on, or the ending of one's physical life, is a shifting from physical awareness to astral awareness, and that awareness already exists and has been living an existence in the afterlife or astral world. The mystic experiences this revelation of beingness in meditation, when disassociated from physical sense perception;

astral perception takes over and reveals this. Almost everyone in our physical world has heard the expression, "living a double life." Well, in the realms of beingness—everyone is living at least a double life.

Yet, realms of one's dimensional existence do not end with simultaneous astral beingness. There are still higher realms of beingness in every human being. There are more ethereal realms of existence that simultaneously exist with these earthly and astral existences, where one's beingness is more angelic or godlike—closer to the Source of life, Universal Mind, Consciousness, or Spirit that is God. Still further into one's beingness are the Christ, Buddha, or Krishna states of conscious beingness, where the individual state of beingness and the Universal are in simultaneous existence.

Consider then that within every human being there are simultaneous states of existence that are active—predating human life, during human life, and beyond human life.

Only when the mental health sciences of today have developed to where they are aware of such simultaneous states of conscious activity can clinical evaluations of such occurrences as psychosis, split personality, and a whole host of other dysfunctions or mental ills be approached and treated from wisdom and true knowledge, rather than only from a limiting, behavioral science or scientific perspective.

On the more productive side, only when a human being is seen as a part of a multidimensional state of beingness can greater productivity, more of one's innate God-given potential, be surfaced to our human conscious awareness. There are vast new frontiers of life existence to be explored, and how exciting to realize that they all already exist within one's self.

Yes, you are many lives being lived simultaneously. The enormity of this reality of your beingness cannot be overstated.

One may then ask—if all this is true, what should I do?

- Live your life as you have, and God's Presence within you will guide you.
- By meditating daily and constantly releasing the false sense of personal will and ego identity that dominates, rather than God's Presence, a higher state of awareness will gradually begin guiding your awareness and life.
- Eventually, whether in this physical lifetime or another, we become aware of the various states of our beingness; and through the grace of God's Presence, we integrate all levels into a harmonious working wholeness of beingness.

It is not impossible—for in absolute truth—all that will be, already is.

Alpha and Omega

When the Christ Mind that was in Jesus spoke the words, "I am the Alpha and Omega—the Beginning and the End" (Rev. 1: 8), a profound mystical truth was being proclaimed, affirming what mystics of the past, present, and future have voiced. The words state that the past (the beginning) and the future (the ending) are as one, and that time, or the appearance of it, is a cosmic blur, an illusion of absolute reality. This is to say that there is no real time lapse between beginning and ending—only the illusion of it. The illusion of time exists to help in the construction of a cosmic duality, where the suggestion of opposites creates the illusion that the one life of the Universe, or God, is now many lives, many lifetimes—all seemingly flowing in time.

The Christ Mind that was in Jesus—aware of the illusion of time and seeing the reality of absolute universal selfhood—made known, to those with spiritual ears to hear, that He existed in a state of universal awareness, of Christ Consciousness existing eternally as Alpha and Omega—beingness without beginning or ending, an endless circle without starting or ending point, an eternity that simply is. Because there is existence, it can be thought of as one eternal moment of time—a cosmic timepiece showing only one moment of time.

Why is all this so important?

Apart from the theological and philosophical implications, the Alpha and Omega reality is not confined to the Christ Presence in Jesus; most importantly, it exists for every human being. Christ Consciousness, the Christ Mind was indeed in Jesus—and it also exists dormant in the unconscious of all men and women. It is that state of consciousness where human manifestation is awake to Universal God Consciousness, eternity, and absolute selfhood—where beginning and ending, Alpha and Omega, are as one. In this state of awareness there are no seeming dualities: conflict is dissolved in the clear light of one state of beingness where all is one, where absolute oneness is not thought about, but experienced as absolute love.

As people live more God-centered lives, they increasingly awaken to the Alpha and Omega within themselves. With increased awakening and as adjustments to a greater reality of life ensue, they become more aware of the illusions of personal ego identity. With those who are old souls or who were awake in previous lives, the true reality can be experienced either to some degree or completely in their present physical lifetimes. To younger souls, the awakening may be gradual over many lifetimes. Always keep in mind, however, that Christ Mind Consciousness already exists in all men and women, so when this or other lifetimes is spoken of, it is merely a point of illusionary reference.

When Paul in the Bible encouraged, "let this mind be in you, which was in Christ Jesus" (Phil. 2: 5), he was in effect encouraging an Alpha and Omega state of consciousness for all humankind to seek. He did not view Alpha and Omega awareness as the sole possession of Jesus. The embodiment of the Christ Mind, Alpha and Omega, was a demonstration of what is in everyone, what everyone can awaken to. Indeed, Jesus was the way-shower to an ever-emerging reality existing in everyone.

It could then be said that everyone is the Alpha and Omega in innermost reality. In the vast majority of souls, it is but a dim light hidden behind the illusion of personal ego identity. Flickers of the light occasionally enter the conscious awareness of some. During such brief periods of inspiration, creativity, or expression, it is as a flower blossoming into full bloom. It beckons to awakening souls that there is a far greater reality to life, and, above all, that they are each an integral part of this greater reality.

The Christ mind that was in Jesus described the Eternity of beingness as Alpha and Omega. Such awakened awareness was also possessed by Buddha, Krishna and others.

Yet, to speculate as to which others possessed it is to repress this knowledge in oneself by being more absorbed by the dualistic appearances of those individual lives and to stray from where one's focus should steadily remain: that everyone, including you in your innermost essence, is the Alpha and Omega.

God has already blessed you with what you already are—and already awakening to.

Souls of Beauty
Dwelling Amongst Us

Idealists dream of a perfect world—a world of peace and harmony where all reflects the beauty of divine life. Can such a world of beauty be contemplated as a possibility? Mystical awareness knows that what may seem to be idealistic wanderings of the imagination might be glimpses into a higher reality.

Anything of a true higher reality brings one's mind closer to Universal Consciousness or God. There are many levels of beingness and souls that correspond to each level, and the Christ Mind that was in Jesus alluded to this mystical reality of beingness in the words, "In my Father's house are many mansions." At each higher level the closeness to the Universal Creative Presence or God draws nearer.

In this physical plane of the planet Earth, there exist souls who have incarnated from a higher level of beingness and are closer to the Ultimate Presence or God. Those who seek wisdom, universal awareness, and enlightenment—the philosophers and true mystics—bring a portion of the Absolute to be expressed to those who are not awake to the profoundness of life on a Universal level of beingness or higher consciousness. Considering this world's population, they are few in numbers, because those who are the seekers are few among the vast number of souls inhabiting the Earth.

There is another soul grouping that inhabits the Earth. Their numbers are larger than that of the mystics' soul grouping, because their expression of the divine is more universal, more easily understood by the soul masses of humanity.

Their message is love.

It is not love of fame, fortune, earthly power, or the all too temporary illusions of worldly life on Earth. Instead, they love the beauty of God expressed in all creation. These souls have incarnated from realms of beingness close to God's Presence, where all is peace, love and harmony—and love of an ethereal nature is seen expressed in the earthly beauty of form, shape, color, sound, and scent. While the word "trouble" exists rampantly throughout the Earth plane, in this other realm, where the beauty of God's Allness permeates throughout, the word "trouble" is nonexistent, for its meaning or experience is unknown. There, ethereally clothed souls of peace, harmony, and love abide, as the beauty of God expresses. These are souls who do not know of war, conflict, and the other dualities that are of earthly plane experience.

Universal Consciousness, Spirit, or God is in a continual process of refinement of all creations, including the endless soul groupings of varying stages of awareness. Thus it is that souls of higher awareness are sent to soul groupings that are lacking such awareness—that they may gradually awaken to a higher divine order of life.

Such a soul grouping can be called souls of beauty. What are the characteristics of such souls?

- They wish to see or acknowledge only good and beauty in the world.
- Their focus is in excluding obvious flaws in others and emphasizing only the good.
- Their positive thinking far surpasses traditional positive thinkers.
- They feel most comfortable surrounded by the natural beauties of nature—the forests, oceans, birds, flowers, and animals. A beautiful sunrise or sunset fills their souls with excitement, for it is a reminder of the tapestry of the higher plane from which they come.
- They do not wish to hear of wars or conflicts. Hence, they are the ones who are accused of "burying their heads in the sand"—not facing physical world realities, living in denial.

In their reality—they love all things of beauty because their very nature is beauty in embodiment. Such beings are souls of beauty—"in this world, not of it," as the Christ Mind in Jesus expressed it. Incarnating into this world, they are a higher energy frequency at their soul level and thus far more sensitive to the experiences of earthly life. Because of this, they are far more easily hurt on a feeling level than souls of a denser, earthly level of soul energy. If they experience hurt there is a strong tendency to retreat from earthly interests and create their own world within a world where they can create beauty of their own making.

As we travel through a physical lifetime, any encounter with souls of beauty can be a blessing. Their very presence, attitude, outlook, and values can brighten your soul's day. You may think them naïve and unrealistic—that earthly life is not like they see it. And yes, you are right—but they are right, too! They are here to refine your soul, to instill into it the seeds of what can be; because, in a realm of beingness, close to God—it already is.

Whenever you are so blessed in your life in encountering a soul of beauty—be exceedingly grateful and thankful, for your soul is being gifted God's beauty, as an oasis in the desert of earthly life.

Yin and Yang—It's Mystical and Power Presence in and Beyond Physical Life

Yin and yang is you—it's me—it's everyone. It is one of the most profound communication symbols of mystical reality upon which the whole of existence exists: it can demonstrate a healing goal sought after in oriental medicine, a philosophical concept to be contemplated, or a mystical symbol to be meditated on.

Yin and yang can indeed be a symbol of many things to many people. Visual symbols have been with mankind since the beginning of recorded history—yet the symbol of yin and yang has held attention to it in a far greater way than other symbols, and for good reason. Most symbols communicate lesser truths—while the symbol of yin and yang communicates life itself.

For life, it symbolizes the manifest and unmanifest—the unmanifesting dark living in the manifesting white—or conversely, the manifesting white existing within the unmanifesting darkness. From a mystical point of view, it can be thought of as the manifesting light, or physical creation's foundation, living within the unmanifesting darkness or Spirit.

Another way to perceive yin and yang is to view the manifesting light and unmanifesting Spirit as forever inseparable. In the words of the Christ Mind in Jesus,

"The Father (unmanifested Spirit Consciousness) and I (the manifesting physical creation) are one."

To put it still another way, we see life manifesting within Spirit, and Spirit manifesting within created life. The Biblical phrase "within Him (God or Universal Spirit Consciousness) we move, live, and have our being" describes humans living in what appears to be a physical universe but which is, in truth, but the physical perceptions of an unmanifest Universal Spirit Consciousness or God.

A symbol such as the yin and yang can be very powerful as a transmitting energy when the symbol itself is physically viewed. The symbol can be viewed as a concentration object before closing one's eyes and entering into a state of meditation. Whether hanging on a wall as a work of art or as some object of art sitting on a table or shrine of some kind, contemplative viewing of the symbol can invoke an awakening in the unconscious, corresponding to its mystical meaning, even without meditating.

The appearance of the yin and yang symbol on clothing in recent years—especially on tee shirts—can be significant in its influence both to the wearer and to those who view it on the wearer. All symbols contain energy lines of force based on the appearance of the symbol. When worn, such energy interacts with the body, mind, and soul energies of the wearer—in this case stimulating the mystical truth within the unconscious. The registering or perception of this stimulation may or may not be apparent to the wearer—although, either way, the mystical/spiritual benefit is there. The same stimulation of mystical oneness between the manifest and the unmanifest can affect others who view this symbol being worn on someone else. Even when worn as smaller physical objects of jewelry such as pendants or rings, the stimulus from the mystical energy can still be at work.

Let the symbol of yin and yang serve you, as it has for so many down through the ages, to awaken mystically and as a harmonic representation of balancing, healing, and wholeness. The visual construction of the symbol invokes a harmonious energy balance in the body, mind, and soul respectively—an interplay and harmonic synthesis of the body with the mind and the mind with the soul, as well as a visual stimulant in healing, wholeness, wellness, and in any practice of a holistic nature.

Ultimately, for the Universe itself to exist, there must be harmony and oneness of interplay and relation between the manifesting and the unmanifesting. The symbol of yin and yang corresponds to this great mystical truth. In an absolute sense the yin and yang symbol is saying, "I am in God and God is in me." There is no truth that is any higher in understanding one's relationship between body, mind, soul, Universal Consciousness, Spirit, or God, for upon this one great mystical truth rests the entirety of physical and human existence.

Be—and live—in the balance of all that is yin and yang.

Union with God—
In Each Other

There is only peace in oneness, and it can rightly be said, there is only love in such oneness. Extending still further—in peace and love that is oneness is allness, and allness can only be described as God.

On this earthly plane of existence there has always been conflict—if not between nations—then certainly with other groups or individuals. Except for a few awake, mystically enlightened souls, this is the way it's been on the earthly plane through history. Certainly there have been periods of peace, but just as certainly, those periods of peace have fallen prey to conflict.

For souls who pray for peace on Earth—take comfort, for there is peace to be found in this universe, but not for the very mass majority on Earth. Mystically understood, there are countless numbers of soul-groupings throughout the universe—both on the physical plane of existence as well as in many other dimensions of existence. Each grouping of souls is at a certain level of awareness spiritually. Each grouping sees and understands each other and God at a certain level of spiritual awareness. Every grouping of souls incarnates into dimensions of energy consciousness that they are in harmonic energy attunement with. There are planes of existence for baby souls, old souls, and for those in between.

Souls who are weighed down by the illusion of personal ego self, generating the illusion of separateness are incarnating into this earthly dimension of existence. This gives way to an illusionary sense of beingness that proclaims something like this: "I am one life, and you are another life," "We share the same planet—but we are two separate existences," "Even if we share the same religion—we are still two different identities," or "The God of my religion is the only true God, and yours is not."

What have all those thoughts in common? All express—separateness. And, wherever there is separateness, the chance for conflict is ever present. Dualities, the illusion of separateness, make up the energy consciousness that is the foundation of Earthly dimensional life. Every soul incarnating here, with exception of higher mystically awakened souls, will continue to incarnate here or to similar planes of existence, incarnation after incarnation until, through experiencing enough conflict and strife, their souls raise to a level of awakening where God's Presence of oneness begins to take over, replacing personal ego and its dualities and separateness with oneness, peace, love—God.

In the earlier stages of this mystical awakening, the soul awakens to union with Spirit or God. In the latter stages of this awakening the soul awakens to union with the same God Presence in others. When such awakened souls leave this earthly plane of existence they find themselves in a grouping of other consciousness-awakened souls. In such a dimension, there are no dualities—only oneness, peace, love, and universal God Presence.

When one prays for lasting peace on Earth, it will never be—but take heart. Worlds of lasting peace do exist. Deep down, hidden in your souls in God's Presence is the knowledge that they do exist—and that is the real stimulus causing one to pray for peace.

In the interim—what to do?

- Realize that you are on this Earth, but ultimately, not of it.
- Realize that you are living in a world created by and of illusion.
- Realize that you are in this world of illusion for a purpose—to ultimately outgrow, more specifically, to reawaken to oneness or God.
- Realize that if you begin to reawaken to the oneness that is God that you must be patient with those who still slumber spiritually. You're on your way back to God, and one day they will be, too.
- Realize with your awakened understanding that such understanding may bring you into conflict with those still under the spell of illusion. Speak of such understanding only with anyone who crosses your path with like understanding. And be certain they truly do have understanding, for

the earthly plane is filled with those who speak of lofty spirituality only to win the confidences of others for their own personal ego gain. In the words of the Christ Mind that was in Jesus, "beware of ravenous wolves in sheep's clothing."

- As you go about your daily business, look at people as souls—rather than physical people. Realize that the very vast majority are caught up in the illusion that they are separate existences. Yet, try to see them as they truly are—souls encased in physical embodiment.

- As you awaken to oneness with God within yourself, awaken to the very same God Presence in others.

- Realize that all ultimate awakening to God's Presence in yourself and others is by grace, we mean that God's Presence is in control of your awakening.

- At an advanced stage of awakening you'll find yourself being more of an observer of earthly life—rather than an emotionally caught up participant.

- Know that you can experience oneness, peace, and life while on this Earth plane by union with God's Presence in yourself. Know that you can only find peace with others on this Earth plane who have awakened mystically to God's Presence within themselves. It is rare on this Earth plane that this happens, but if it does, consider it a bit of heaven on Earth.

Only in a dimension where soul-groupings are all

mystically awakened to the same life presence of God can the much sought after environment of lasting peace, love, oneness—God's Presence—be a reality. Till such time, even if it's only a philosophical statement of belief, acknowledge that God's Presence is the ultimate—and in reality—the only life in others.

May God's Presence guide you through the illusions of separateness into the eternal light of oneness.

Self-Will versus Destiny

On this earthly plane of existence, humanity exists in a cosmic house of mirrors. What seems to be reality is, in truth, but an illusion of limited five-sense perception. If one is to understand one's own life—one must understand life itself. And to do this, a person must be able to discern what is real from that which is not.

Through recorded history the subject of will has played a significant role. The idea of exerting one's personal will to make things happen in one's life plays a major part in giving value or existence to the false sense of personal ego identity. Many books and commentaries have applauded the use of will power to accomplish goals in life. Exerting one's will over others is often suggested as a means to an end. The world is filled with countless people who are going through the motions of pushing forth through life by what they believe is the power of their personal wills.

For a moment let's suppose that some persons believe that their self-wills are causing them to accomplish what they are in life. Of course, to have self-will necessitates basing one's identity on a false sense of personal ego selfhood: A person is thought to be one self or identity—and others are seen to be different personal identities. Thinking in this fashion means that one's mind is accepting that everyone is separate from one another.

Further, mental acceptance of separateness causes division amongst people, which, in turn, opens the doorway to disagreements or conflicts. What this means, however, is that even if some individuals were successful and crediting their successes to will power— they would still not be fulfilled or feel whole in spite of their worldly measures of success, due to living in a state of separateness. So even if such persons think that they are successful by worldly standards, they are still feeling a sense of lack or threatened by other separate selves— each using personal will to possibly dethrone the success.

So it would look to most that the seeming exertion of personal self-will, while seeming to produce results, is not really producing a lasting fulfillment and peace within a person's soul because of a sense of separateness. And, mystically, there is a reason for this: the personal ego identity does not really exist except as an illusion of the outer senses. But more directly to the point, if the personal ego self does not exist, how then can something nonexistent produce a power that can be presented as a "doing" power known as will-power or self-will?

In mystical reality there cannot be self-will because there is no real personal self to generate it. So, if some people seem to produce results in life, but those results and will power are only an illusion, what else could be present to account for strides or advances in one's life?

Enter—destiny.

Does the soul have a destiny, and is it really destiny rather than the illusion of self-will to which credit should be given?

Of course, destiny conjures up predestination. Predestination rightly suggests a future that is preordained—or, more specifically, a future that already is. To state it another way, in God's cosmic clock of time—the future is preordained because past, present, and future make up one singular moment of time.

In mystical reality every soul has already lived successes that they mistakenly give credit to self-will for.

In mystical or absolute reality there is but one Life in this Universe—hence any will that exists is the Will of One Universal Life or God. Whatever good happens in life is by the Will or Grace of God. Whatever is, by worldly measure, the opposite of good, is a result of separateness from one's source for good or—God.

One may ask, then, why is it that so-called evil people with immense separateness and super-egotistical wills flourish by worldly standards? Actually, they have nothing to do with their successes. Certain souls have reached levels of consciousness where they need to experience extreme materialism so that they may vanquish such cravings, allowing their souls to progress to higher spiritual states. These souls are also used as examples, demonstrating to other souls that physical plane material achievement will, in the final analysis, not bring fulfillment.

The Christ Mind that was in Jesus responded to this same question in the simple yet profound words, "What profit a man if he gain the whole world and lose his own soul?" The soul can be described as one's spiritual connection to the eternal or God. Without such a connection, the soul becomes what could be described as a lost soul, roaming aimlessly through existence after existence, trying to use an imaginary will power or self-will to find lasting happiness, lasting fulfillment, and lasting peace—but they are illusive.

If all is already—and there is but the Will of God— why is all this illusion allowed to take place?

Because without the illusion of separate identities and the byproduct of self-will, the Universal one life of God would remain one life without creation—human life or other forms of life. The one life that is God creates the illusion of many lives or separate selves living within an illusion of time. Creation gives the appearance of being created at different times. Yet in reality only one life and one moment of eternal time really exists. Because of the illusion of time, souls give the appearance of being created at various times—hence we have baby souls, old souls, and those in-between. In the eternal maturity of God there is a purpose to it all.

In the dualities of separateness, love or oneness is highlighted as being far more valuable than separateness and resultant loneliness. Evil based on extreme separateness further demonstrates the value of Goodness. It highlights the choice to be made in the human soul—the choice between darkness, separation, and destruction or light, oneness, love and God.

The futility of the illusion of self-will or will power yields itself to the reality of oneness and the truth that, in the beginning, which is one and the same as the ending, there is only God's Will: that the path of every created soul can, of reality, lead to God's Oneness—for in absolute reality it has never been separated from God, as alluded to in the Bible: "Within Him (God), we move and live and have our being."

In summation—there cannot be an opposition of self-will versus destiny, for self and its will do not really exist, and destiny is a future that already exists.

It is God's Will to create the illusion and fill it with souls, so that each soul in the illusion might come to an awakening of the eternal moment and give acknowledgement of God's Existence—that the one life allness of all in all may convey the presence, "I am that, that I am."

The Sacredness
of Silence

There's a mystical expression that goes, "He who speaks more knows less, and he who speaks less knows more." If one encounters religious zealots, they are very likely to speak at great length and volume about their beliefs. A person who is advanced in spiritual awareness knows to remain silent and let the zealot ramble on. With awareness, one knows that to try to enlighten such a person at this level of awareness would do no good. It would only end in a meaningless debate. There's nothing to be gained. Better to remain silent, being content to know that in some future lifetime every zealot will awaken to a much greater realization of spiritual truth.

All who have studied deeper forms of meditation for the purpose of experiencing mystical union with God do all they can to enter into the silence of the absolute. Only when the mind can be totally quieted can absolute presence be known. As long as thinking occupies the mind—God cannot. Thoughts and thinking are all activities of the false sense of personal ego identity. Even those thoughts that dwell on God are still part of personal ego consciousness. As long as the personal ego is active, even in the loftiest of ways, God's Presence remains unknown.

Mystics of higher awareness through the ages have taught that personal ego thoughts have to be totally stilled so that God may be known. As a result all kinds of systems have been developed to achieve such silence. Most systems revolve around what, decades ago, I described as the exhaustion principle—that is, exhaust the mind so that the thinking process gives way to silence wherein the sacredness of God's Presence can be known. One example can be seen in an exhaustive dance where the dancers so deplete themselves that they collapse and the body/mind relationship (without the personal ego energy) takes over. That is—exhaust the body and you exhaust the personal ego level of the mind; and if consciousness remains, it is only the sacred silence of the eternal or God.

The Biblical words that express it all are, "Be still and know that I am God." So many turn to God daily, seeking God's guidance or some form of divine intervention in their lives, yet they cannot hear God's Presence for it is drowned out by the loudness of their thoughts. The Christ Mind that was in Jesus referred to this as "praying amiss." Simply put, the more one prays using thought—the less one can hear the Voice of the Silence (God). Candidly, the only time prayer makes a connection to God or Universal Presence is when the personal ego has exhausted itself or let go, and in letting go creates a consciousness void which is instantly filled with God's Universal Presence. To the very heart of the matter, if a person never uttered a word of prayer, but simply became as silent as possible, Universal Presence or God would respond. In other words, a person does not have to ask, as expressed from the Christ Mind that was in Jesus through the words, "your Father knows what you have need of—before you ask."

In the sacred silence of God's Universal Presence, all is already known—inclusive of all souls—both in the seen physical world and in the unseen world of other dimensions, for past, present, and future co-exist in one eternal moment of time. And, it must be noted that whatever a person would be moved to pray for will not be answered as a physical reality if it is not what is best for the soul's journey at any given so-called time in the soul's journey, without beginning or ending through Eternity.

If we wish to be more under the influence of the Universal Presence of God, may we speak less outwardly and listen more inwardly. There's an expression that goes, "he is a man of few words." When such a person is encountered, in most instances when the person does speak, the words are meaningful and insightful. When that person doesn't speak, whether consciously aware of it or not, the silence opens some degree of receptivity to and influence by the knowingness of universal God Presence.

Health is so very important—so please also note that one's health can be greatly influenced by the sacred silence of God's Presence. Whenever you begin to have a feeling that something is not right with the health of the body, if at all possible, you should become as quiet as possible. Granted this may not always be possible if extreme pain or other discomfort is present—but as soon as it has diminished be as quiet and still as possible, both physically and mentally. If possible enter a meditative state—even a light one will do. This will give greater presence for the primal energy of universal God Presence to work on adjusting all the out-of-balance energy factors in your body and mind, thereby restoring the energy factors and improving health. When it comes to health and healing, indeed silence is golden, for it is the sacred silence of universal God Presence working to maintain or restore the health of one's body.

Being quieter, more silent also allows the power and love of God's Presence to be more easily experienced by others. Many years ago, I knew of a man who was married to a very bright and beautiful woman who, in her enthusiasm for life, talked and talked to an extreme. One day, he asked her to engage in an experiment of not speaking for a few minutes. The wife became silent. After a few minutes the husband said to her, "When you are silent I feel an enlargement of your presence. I sense a greater beauty, power, and love emanating forth from you. I feel a greater sense of a wonderful you that I cannot sense when I'm concentrating on your words. I can be aware of the truer, deeper you, and it's wonderful." From that day forward the wife spoke less, because when she was silent, she too could sense a greater presence—the sacred silence of God's Presence filling her soul.

Yes, whether it be affecting one's health, a relationship, or, most importantly, one's entire life, the sacred silence of God's Universal Presence is there within all—awaiting the quieting of thoughts and thinking.

Be still then—enter the sacred silence of God's Presence and know the blessings of God's peace and love.

The Jesus Complex—or Claims to Be Jesus—Mystically Understood

Uncertainty, war, fear, confusion, ill health, loneliness—these are just a few of the reasons people often welcome someone who might claim to be Jesus in the physical flesh. The Christ Mind that was in Jesus warned that there would be those who would appear in his name. And certainly there have been. People who are particularly hurting, for reasons already stated, are open and vulnerable to someone handing them a business card with the single name of Jesus on it.

Of course, it takes more than a business card. It takes giving the outer appearance of what people would believe Jesus should look like. If you have ever seen any movie about the life of Jesus, you know that the actor who gets the role looks like what people have, from childhood's conditioning, believed him to look like. If there were a casting call by a movie producer for an actor to play Jesus, the requirements might be as follows:

Wanted – Actor to Play Jesus

- Must have long hair, at least shoulder length
- Must have a warm, pleasing smile
- Must be physically attractive and charismatic

- Must be able to present a gentleness, yet be firm when necessary
- If with blue eyes, they must be bright, piercing, and engaging
- If with dark or brown eyes, they must be soulful, compassionate, and penetrating

Now for a moment, imagine that the role of Jesus was not being cast for a movie—but someone had chosen himself to play out such a role in real life. The most obvious move would be to look the part: stop a few haircuts, check out colored contact lenses, and see a good dentist for a wonderful loving smile. And, let's not forget dress. No one expects Jesus to arrive in a business suit. Allowing that a robed look might be too much over the top, the final look should be casual—a simple, uncomplicated attire, for that too is something people would expect of Jesus.

The personality should be gentle, loving, and forgiving, especially of those who may not believe that he is Jesus. The Jesus personality must also be able to speak in a manner of authority—as one who truly knows and is Jesus.

Next is the religious or spiritual part. This person, because of spiritual study or lack thereof, may take a fundamentalist Christian view, quoting often from the Bible, or an esoteric approach, relying on teachings of mystics through the ages. Whichever the choice—fundamentalist Christian beliefs or esoteric Christian interpretations—there will be a ready audience of souls with enough vulnerability to make them easy recruits for one claiming to be the reappearing Jesus. There will even be a few learned academics who will be lured in. Anyone claiming to be Jesus loves this, as he can point out that even those who are learned accept him as Jesus.

Reference for Those Claiming to Be Jesus

There are so many who have made the claim to be Jesus. For an interesting description of the various claimants, go to the Internet to Wikipedia under: List of people claiming to be Jesus.

Knowing Imposter or Self-deluded?

If a person knows that he is not the real Jesus having come back and is simply taking advantage of people for his own ends, he can still be convincing to his acquired followers.

Or, the person can genuinely believe himself to be Jesus. But what would cause such self-delusions?

Both the knowing imitator and the genuinely self-deluded have the presence of Christ Energy Consciousness within them. When speaking, they both unconsciously can draw—not from Jesus' Beingness—but from Christ Energy, which is within everyone, both saint and sinner.

The fundamentalist will communicate this Christ

energy in a more unsophisticated manner—while the esoteric one will present more of an ethereal, otherworldly form of expression. Of the two, the latter is the more convincing—because even if people don't understand what is being said, his manner of expression elevates the Jesus figure as someone who knows of the higher things of God. Eventually, both the knowing imposter and the self-deluded Jesus will implode—for the truth that neither is really Jesus will come out.

Subtle Imitations

In today's world there are far more who do not claim to be Jesus than those who do. Without saying they are Jesus, they will attempt to project a Jesus image to their followers. Review the casting-call image of Jesus, and, you may find someone who has played or is playing the role by image projecting. Remember always the popular saying, "what you see is not necessarily what you get."

Reincarnated Jesus Followers

Adding to the fragile credibility of one claiming to be Jesus are those among the followers who attempt to verify that he is Jesus; they claim they knew him when he was the historical Jesus. They could claim to have been anyone. Most prominent seem to be the many who have claimed to be Mary Magdalene. On a purely false, personal ego-centered consciousness, claiming to have known the person who claims to be Jesus gives that person status or elevates him or her above the other followers in the group. Through this method of association one adds to one's own false sense of personal ego identity, even developing an obsession, wherein the reincarnated follower truly believes this reality. This belief generally will win added favor with the Jesus claimant, for it appears to strengthen his claim to be the claimed reincarnation.

The Greater, More Important Mystical Reality

What's the great lesson to be learned from all this? Mystically, all of us carry Christ Conscious energy in our innermost beings. However, there are times when this so dominates a consciousness that the person could fall prey to believing that he or she is Jesus. Nor, as pointed out previously, are they not Jesus. For they are experiencing the same energy consciousness as Jesus had in his day. When a person is in such a state of mind—he or she is in a Christ Mind state of awareness, and concepts, ideals, and love can flow forth from him or her the same as it did from the historical Jesus.

From a mystical interpretation, the following words from the Bible reinforce the reality of the energy of Christ Consciousness in everyone:

- 1 Corinthians 3:23 "And ye are Christ's; and Christ is God's."
- 1 Corinthians 2:16 "But we have the Mind of Christ."
- Philippians 2:5 "For let this mind be in you, which was also in Christ Jesus."

However, when one has truly awakened to God's Presence within—one is not impressed by anyone claiming to be Jesus. But by having awakened to Christ Consciousness within oneself, one may share the emerging wisdom without any claims to be Jesus or anyone else in the history of religion that people would tend to look up to.

It is not the messenger—but the message that is important. All messengers, including Jesus, pass quickly from physical view, but the message, which is timeless, lives forever.

True spiritual messengers/teachers do not have to pretend or regard themselves as some great historical figure—they stand on the message alone.

Be thankful for such messengers and respect them for the Christ Consciousness Energy that speaks through them—but don't worship them, saving worship for God's Presence within yourself.

Living in and by Mystical Grace

Every day that we awaken from sleep, it is by grace. To take a breath and to be alive is not by an act of personal ego will, but because of grace. Some people may argue that their personal egos' wills caused them to survive some difficult time in their lives, but it was not—that was only the illusion. In truth we survive by grace; it was not yet our cosmic time to surrender our physical existence in the ultimate cosmic scheme of things, where nothing is by chance or coincidence and where all is perfectly orchestrated in a harmonious cosmic melody.

So often the phrase, "by the grace of God," is used by people, but what is its meaning? Its obvious meaning is that something has happened or will happen because Universal Presence or God allowed it to happen or will allow it to happen. Grace could then be thought of as the Will of God—not the personal ego's will—having supreme or ultimate power over all things and human existence, and even life itself.

When atheists "worship" evolution as the chance coincidence explaining the origin and sustaining of life, that viewpoint is also, when mystically understood, an outcome of universal grace. There is a divine

Orchestration to life. Whether life showed up as a result of evolution, from beings from outer space, or as another dimensional space, it matters not, because existence, no matter how it exists, is so by grace.

To be conscious or to have consciousness is by grace. It is not by chance or coincidence—more again, it is by grace.

The Importance

Apart from being engrossed in mystical philosophy and psychology as to the nature and origin of one's life, the knowledge and knowing of the grace of the Universe, Universal Presence or God, is of utmost importance in living one's life. It can be the ultimate difference-maker in how one's life is lived. When a person lives in a state of consciousness such that there is the awareness that all taking place is by the grace of God, there is peace in one's surface, outer mind. More importantly, that peace in the outer-mind level emanates from a deeper level of one's soul.

The Illusion and the Reality

If a prayer seems to work it is not because of the prayer, but by grace; or it worked because the prayer was in accord and harmony with the Will of God. In other words, that's how everything would have turned out, whether the prayer had been given or not. The very same can be said of visualizations, affirmations, and all similar spiritual practices.

What an insult to one's false personal ego identity!

When one prays, visualizes, and so on, it is the false personal ego identity that's involved trying to affirm or beg God to do something. The personal ego thinks that it is doing something. This belief satisfies in many the illusionary importance of the personal ego and existence. On the other hand one who is humble before God also may pray with all good intentions and as a result of love. Regardless, the outcome comes about as a result of grace or God's Will.

The Christ Mind that was in Jesus also echoed the knowing of grace in the Words, "not my Will—but thine be done." Or in the words, "Why callest thou me good? There is none good but one, that is, God."

If all is by grace why then do prayer, affirmations, visualizations, and other such spiritual practices exist? Because through such practices human consciousness reminds itself of the existence, presence, power of God and God's Will, and ultimately—that all is as a result of grace or the Will of God.

When someone passes on, it could be thought of as the grace of time for this lifetime, for the good of the soul on this Earth plane has passed, and it is time for the good of the soul to, by grace—move on. By grace, there is a greater glory that awaits a departing soul than that which can be known on this physical plane of existence.

So, if a person passes on but another person has

been praying for that person to stay physically present, remember that it is by grace the passing occurred for the good of the departing soul. Know that it was by grace that one experienced some life with that soul, that all that was felt in the heart emanated from the spiritual heart of love of God, and that the departing person had been a gift from God or by grace.

Want to know more about what life is really about? Then always try to focus in on the bigger picture—the universal life process or simply the Will of God. Prayer, visualization, affirmations are good because they are reminders of God's Presence and Power to create life and be the source of our every breath, for again—all is by grace.

What to Do?

If, in spite of what has been said, a person is still moved to pray, visualize and affirm, do so; for every soul must follow or yield to his or her spiritual understanding or awareness. And, along with being a reminder of grace, as previously mentioned, the following could occur:

- When the tears are no more, or the need satisfied, there is a peace that comes when all the prayer that can be uttered at the time has been spoken and only the Presence of God remains.

- You may exhaust your mind through visualization and imaging, which is good, for in exhaustion there is a release and, thus, a turning over to God.

- You may, through repetitive affirmations, lose track of your words, and if they run into each other in a meaningless fashion, there is then nothing left to do but to let go and turn it over to God.

All of these possibilities are a reminder of the limitation of a false personal ego's sense of identity—and all are totally reliant on the Power and Grace of God.

In love, I share with you the following words of mystical awareness as they were—by grace—gifted to me:

I let go and let God, that by grace, the greatest good has been done and already is.

The Beginning
of Wisdom

The first step to wisdom is to admit you know nothing. Yet, until one is ready, this is almost an impossible thing to admit. The false personal ego identity, which may make claim to knowing so much, rebels when considering that all its thoughts add up to nothing. It does not matter whether the accumulation of what one believes to be knowledgeable has been gathered through the practical experience of daily life, through formal education, or through religious teachings. All is stored up in a make-believe identity of the personal ego, which prides itself that it is a storehouse of such knowledge.

Yet, such accumulated knowledge is not to be classified as wisdom. A person may be quite knowledgeable by worldly standards—yet totally lacking in wisdom. For any person who possesses wisdom—and there are but a few on this physical Earth dimension—there is an awareness that goes beyond being knowledgeable.

Until we can empty our consciousness of any belief that what we know has any significant value in the eternal scheme of things, there can be no release to wisdom. As most people base their identities on their accumulated knowledge, to challenge such knowledge is to challenge their sense of identity or existence, as they perceive it. The greater such accumulated knowledge, the greater the task to declare, "For all I know—I know nothing." For, again, the false sense of personal ego identity is threatened.

Empirical evidence, such as double-blind studies, can be classified as knowledge—but not wisdom. Knowledge accumulated through human reason, logical deduction, or analysis is not wisdom. It is temporary knowledge, which may not stand the test of so-called time. Today's science can readily become tomorrow's superstition.

But wisdom is a timeless presence. When mystics seek guidance from God, it is wisdom that is active in their consciousness. Then, the personal ego mind, with its accumulated knowledge, is looked upon as a toolbox, with its contents to be directed by wisdom. In other words, whatever appears in the consciousness of true mystics is intuitively directed by Universal Mind/Spirit/God, showing them how and what to use from the false personal ego's toolbox. This is the opposite of false personal egos (or the collection of the false personal ego) trying to figure out how they should use their accumulated content. That usage is more like the expression, "the tail wagging the dog."

To the mystic, the accumulated knowledge contained in the false personal ego identity and its support of such identity are the greatest obstacles to wisdom. For, however much personal ego knowledge has been accumulated, that amount can increase the barrier to wisdom. Those academics and scientists who purely worship the scientific method, can oftentimes, to an observer, seem, as the expression goes—full of themselves. It is not uncommon to hear a disgruntled patient who has been talked down to, express the words, "Who does he think he is—God?"

Even supposed, elevated spiritual knowledge is not wisdom. The false personal ego still plays in the schoolyard of intellect (that is, nothing posing as something) in a make-believe world of outer sense perceptions.

In contrast, having wisdom is living in a state of humbleness and co-operation. The humbleness comes from knowing that the only real existence is Universal Mind/Spirit/God. It is an awareness that only God knows. Human consciousness and awareness stand naked and humbled by the Magnificence that is the allness. The shackles of false outer identity have fallen away, and the soul stands before Spirit in spiritual nudity.

Living then becomes a matter of cooperating with universal reality or universal consciousness. To do so, in effect, is to be gladly a channel of God's Will. Every day of life is lived openly, receiving direction intuitively from God's Presence as to what to do and how to do it. All accumulated knowledge is no longer under the control of a false personal ego identity. That knowledge is now the exclusive property of Universal Mind/Spirit/God, to be directed and controlled by Universal Presence.

In such a state of conscious awareness a wise person lives each day—living in and by wisdom, in a state of mind wishing to co-operate with the directives of Universal Presence. Wisdom, then, is the light that one walks in when reawakened to the greater reality of the One Life/Mind/Spirit/God of Universal Presence.

The few on this Earth plane of existence who have wisdom are oftentimes hard to distinguish from others. They do not pass among others with a smug aura of superiority. That stance is for those presenting themselves as the accumulators of knowledge warehoused in a false personal sense of ego identity. In fact, each would just as soon blend in, going quietly, as the Christ Mind that was in Jesus said, "about my Father's business."

What to do?

As originally stated, first there is the admission that, for all you know (the accumulated knowledge of the false sense of personal ego), you know nothing. Then, do all you can do spiritually to prove it. Once again, in the words of the Christ Mind that was in Jesus, "...the words that I speak unto you I speak not of myself: but the Father that dwelleth in me, He doeth the works" (John 14:10, KJV).

Wisdom is a rapture of consciousness between the finite and the Infinite. With the discarding of nothing, everything will be left to fill the void; and with the influence and presence of everything, wisdom exists.

The Effectiveness and Non-Effectiveness of Spiritual Practices

Do prayers, visualizations, affirmations or other spiritual practices really work, or if they only work sometimes, why?

This question is asked repeatedly by many—those who ask for prayer and those who pray or use some other spiritual practice for themselves or others. With the progression in spiritual awakening, the answers change.

As an example, in the old-time, basic fundamentalist religion, prayer for most is a pleading, begging, or hoping for some desired result. As a person moves in spiritual awareness to a higher plane of consciousness or understanding, such as that of New Thought or basic metaphysics, the pleading and begging cease, and prayer becomes an affirming that, through God's Power, the desired effect is already so.

The question then becomes, which is most effective: old-fashioned prayer or newer New Thought prayer? If truth be told, both can be effective—and, at the least, give that illusion of effectiveness to one's personal perception. Or, on the other hand, whether one uses traditional, New Thought, or any other spiritual practice, the results can prove to be ineffective.

Why is this? Does God favor one person or religion over another? The answer found in all results is that God has no favorites.

Why, then?

For a moment, become reflective and ask yourself this question: What if every prayer were answered favorably and every other form of spiritual practice brought about the requested result?

Keep also in mind that the initiation of most spiritual practices is for the betterment of one's own condition in some way, without thought of others. During such times, the false personal sense of ego identity, with limited awareness, attempts to influence God as to what to do. If everyone received exactly what was prayed for, visualized for, or affirmed for, would humankind then live in a perfect world?

Whether individuals engage in any spiritual practices for the good of one person or even the entirety of creation, they still do not even begin to have the awareness necessary concerning the final result. Instead of a perfect world, there would be chaos! The reality is that humankind collectively, as it exists in consciousness on this physical plane of existence, does not possess sufficient awareness to truly know what to ask for or desire. Only Universal Presence, or God, knows what is best for any one person—or the totality of universal existence.

The answer?

From God's vantage point within the innermost consciousness of every soul, Universal Presence knows when to respond and when not to, which is, in and of itself, a response. At all times, God or Universal Presence knows what is best for the individual soul's eternal existence and for all souls manifesting collectively as humanity on the physical Earth plane of existence.

Universal Consciousness, Presence, or God, as Creator and Sustainer, recognizes that all that is taking place everywhere must be in harmony and balance on a Universal scale. Without harmony and balance, as previously stated, chaos would ensue throughout the physical and other-dimensional universe. To grant the requested results to everyone who used some manner of spiritual practice to bring about some desired result, without awareness of how such a result would set up a Universal chain reaction, would be pure folly.

When any spiritual practice is in attunement and alignment with Universal Will, results will seem to take place. The lack of results will seem to be the outcome when the spiritual practice is not in attunement and alignment with Universal Presence or God's Will. Keep in mind that this is true whenever the false personal sense of ego identity is engaged in any spiritual practice and that Universal Presence or God is totally in control—at all times.

There comes a time in the life of every soul that an emptying out of personal ego takes place, with the subsequent replacement by universal God Presence Consciousness. The intention is to bring the energy field of the soul's human manifestation into greater harmony, balance, or alignment with manifesting Universal Energy or Universal God Consciousness/Spirit. In this way, it is Universal Consciousness or God entering into the awakening person's surface frontal consciousness that creates the prayer, visualization, affirmation, or other spiritual practice—and the personal ego is less and less involved.

- It is then God who creates the prayer that is prayed.
- It is then God who visualizes the visualization.
- It is then God who affirms the affirmations.
- It is then God who is directing any other spiritual practice.

As this emptying out is always a work in progress while the soul is in human form, this alteration is not taking place 100% of the so-called time. Occasionally, because of the illusions of sense perceptions, the false personal ego might appear in control. But as universal awareness, Christ-Mindedness, or its equivalent gains more control, those momentary lapses become fewer.

Summing up:

Suffering, whether in oneself or in others, cries out for relief, and it is a human reflex to pray, visualize, affirm, or engage in spiritual practice. Eventually the suffering will subside, whether by healing or seeming death (soul transition). In the interim, chaos is avoided and universal existence is saved; the soul, as a result, enjoys the beauty of harmony and balance within itself and all that surrounds it.

Always keep in awareness that Universal Presence is eternally in control for the ultimate good of every soul. And so, what will be, will be—because it already is.

Mystically Living in a Threatening World

- Superbugs increasingly resistant to antibiotics!
- Stays in hospitals becoming riskier!
- Planetary pollution of the oceans and waterways!
- Electrical energies flood the airwaves, affecting energy fields of the human body!
- Instant mass-media transmission of horrors and destruction!
- Fears of terrorism mounting worldwide!
- Predictions of a failing U.S. economy and its impact on world economies!
- A resurgence of the threat of nuclear annihilation!

News occurs instantly and constantly throughout our world, both about our planet and our fellow inhabitants being threatened in so many ways. And, it is rare if people do not go about their daily business feeling threatened in one or more ways—whether this threat be conscious or festering slightly beneath the surface level of awareness. Most individuals just live against a threatening backdrop, as does their concern for those they dearly love.

Now, certainly, throughout the world's history

people have felt threatened by others or their environment. Yet today people feel more threatened than at any time in the past due to the instant transference of news. In the past, it took time for the news to catch up to people. Now it's there in an instant—moments after it happened or even while it is happening. It is no longer a rarity to hear and see the announcement of "breaking news." Certainly there are some positive news stories—but those warm-hearted expressions of the divine are fewer as media time is consumed with news of the lesser part of the psyche creating havoc.

In such a world of instant, breaking news, increasing numbers of people are opting out of watching television, especially that which is news related. Some are actually ridding themselves of their televisions and other receiving devices. Yet, technology continues to mushroom, while the psyche or human mind/soul lags further and further behind. The result, sadly, is a greater power for destruction, with human consciousness on this earthly physical plane of existence unable to control it.

Why, then, should there not exist breeding grounds for new, spiritually clothed leaders to show up with promises of hope that the world is about to be spiritually transformed into a peaceful and higher existence? When so many threats are present, people would flock to such messengers of hope, whether the message be a second coming, the reappearance of a messiah, a galactic arrival, a global energy shift, a rapture, or a combination of any of the aforementioned. Yes, through fear of so many threats, it is easy for spiritual hucksters to gather around them a flock of followers desperate for good news, security, and safety.

The purpose of *Mystical Insights* is to deal with reality—life on this physical plane of existence as it really is—not as it seems and not as how peaceful and loving souls might wish it to be.

This is not a planet that souls incarnate onto to experience peace, but to awaken over countless lifetimes to the eternal peace that they are a part of. The Bible correctly states, "There is a time for war and a time for peace," and this has been the history on this physical dimension of planetary existence over and over again. As a result, people who are caught up in earthly life may view those who have carried homemade signs proclaiming, "The end is near" as self-deluded and mentally disturbed—and that viewpoint has eventually proved itself to be true.

Oh, for the days of Atlantis, Lemuria, Mu, or some other civilization that once inhabited this earthly physical plane of existence! For all their rumored advancements, why are they still not present?

So—what to do?

This physical, earthly plane of existence, existing as it does, is a dualistic house of smoke and mirrors. Personal existences do not really exist at all. All is based on a sense of personal ego existence where all seems divided into many. And, where there is the illusion of many, that diversity of soul levels causes conflict. Where there is conflict—there is always the presence of feeling threatened.

First, realize that this feeling of threat—wars, strife, conflict, or the constant threat of all of those—is the way it is, has been, and will always be on this physical, earthly plane of existence.

- Second, at this point of your soul's awakening, be at peace with God as you know God to be. Rather than become totally caught up in the energy illusions of this physical plane activity and all its "breaking news," take time to break into the higher levels of consciousness within yourself through deeper, more mystical forms of meditation. Seek the mystical "Peace of God that passeth all understanding"—the heavenly Universal God Consciousness within yourself. Take to heart the mystical meaning of the words from the Bible: "know ye not that ye are the temple of God?" Here, within your soul, you'll find the Eternal, lasting Peace that you seek in the one life Universal Consciousness of God Presence.

- Third, on an outer daily basis when interacting with others, constantly forgive them their ignorance. For they are no different than you, only less awakened to what really is and what really is not. They are all expressions of the one life of which we are all a part. The words coming forth from the Christ Mind that was in Jesus spoke of this, as his body was hanging on the cross: "Forgive them, Father, they know not what they do."

- Fourth, although you may certainly feel that it is difficult to love others, especially when "breaking news" speaks of their atrocities and inhumane acts, yet, mystically realize that there are souls that incarnate to this physical Earth plane that have come straight from hellish dimensions of existence to which they will return time and time again. Mystically speaking, life on this physical Earth plane of existence for the majority of its inhabitants is the initial stage of re-awakening. Those that singularly do heinous acts towards others are experiencing surfaced remnants of the lower hellish past.

- Fifth, know that finally, ever so slowly, they will awaken to the greater reality that pain and suffering are not the eternal way of life—but the peace of the eternal one life of Universal Presence is.

- Finally, realize that when you hear crowds of people screaming "death to this country or that country or that race," they are being driven by someone taking the role of a divider in order to create a common enemy and deflect attention from that leader's own failings—lest the leader be found out, and fall from power. Quite simply, the dividers of this world divide people, and, in so doing, distance the populace from awakening to the Presence of One Life Universal or God.

This earthly, physical plane of existence will always have drama—up to its final dramatic moment when it is no more. In the interim, during any lifetime here on this physical dimension of Earth, render unto Earth your physical body and the eternal existence of your soul to eternal existence or God.

As you might say if this were your last day on Earth, start every day with the words, "I give up my soul to the eternal light of God Presence." In this way you'll find it far easier to live through this lifetime of threatening existence.

"Yea, though I walk through the valley of the shadow of death, I will fear no evil, for thou art with me; thy rod and thy staff they comfort me . . . surely goodness and mercy shall follow me all the days of my life: and I will dwell in the house of the Lord forever."

To rise above life's drama, live a God-centered life.

Rituals—Till God Fills the Void that Never Was

Since the beginning of recorded time, rituals have been engaged in by various religious and spiritual groups. To many, they form some sort of bridge between themselves and the divine or God. From very simple people living meagerly in huts to the so-called captains of industry at the top of skyscrapers, very few people are immune from finding themselves engaged in some form of religious ritual. In many religions, rituals take up a great deal of the followers' time.

To the vast majority of souls occupying this Earth plane of existence, some sort of ritual is practiced in accord with the general theology espoused. The question should be asked—if so much time is taken in the practice of rituals, are they of any real value? Is there anything to be gained from rituals, or are they just part of pomp and circumstance to impress the masses?

Mystically speaking:

Rituals are performed as an outer spiritual practice simply because a person does not know about stepping into the inner spiritual communion of spirit.

It seems that most larger religious bodies rely on rituals. Rituals are easier for people to engage in and, for those in charge, to manipulate or hold in check large masses of followers. To put it another way, the more advanced any spirituality may be, the fewer the followers or need for rituals.

Rituals, mystically speaking, are used till they are no longer of any consequence for the sake of one's spirituality. In fact, at a certain point of spiritual awakening rituals become an interference to higher spiritual awakening.

Why go through the ritualistic motions when non-motion or silence opens the door of consciousness to Universal Mind/Spirit Presence—God? To a person who has achieved mystical awareness of universal God Presence, rituals are at a level of sandbox spirituality. But why, if rituals are at such a childish level of spirituality, are they allowed to continue? What is their purpose or value?

Rituals do have a role in one's life until such time as a soul reunites in consciousness with Spirit. Like any religion that God or Universal Presence allows to exist, its purpose is for some collective entity or group of people to be reminded of Universal Presence at their very basic level of understanding. The symbolism of rituals causes them to feel that they are doing something spiritual. In fact, they are, on the simplest of consciousness levels, acknowledging that God exists. Even souls on a basic level of spirituality are stimulated from within to acknowledge outwardly what their souls already know inwardly. Ritualistic religions offer such very young souls the opportunity to acknowledge that a higher Presence—God—created them. This doing something or being in motion satisfies the personal ego, and, in a sense, gives the soul some relief from the false personal sense of identity.

Rituals seem to fill the void of illusionary time that never really was. When one awakens spiritually to the ultimate truth, one realizes that the void that never really was has been, in reality, always filled with the Eternal. The further one awakens spiritually, the less doing—and the more being.

It should be pointed out that there are rituals for good, which are to acknowledge God, and there are, unfortunately, rituals for the not so good—or carried to an extreme, rituals that can be described as evil.

Those that engage in rituals to bring about control for personal gain at the expense of others or for power over others or to cause torment or destruction of others are at the height of self-delusion. Why? Because they believe that their false personal ego is their true identity. They practice rituals to call upon the illusionary power that caters to those clinging to the false ego identity. They are caught up in what can only be described as vain, self-absorbed, egotism. They seek power from the illusionary power of rituals, for there is no power within the false sense of personal ego identity. The leaders of such groups play on the vulnerability of souls who are lost in the illusionary mazes of false ego identities. In such an atmosphere, rituals dominate—which should speak volumes about rituals: the more rituals dominate in any group, the further away they are from the Universal One Life of God. The only thing that is accomplished from rituals without good intent is to dredge up primitive archetypal energies from the past and let them create remembrances of an even greater divide from the One Life Presence of God.

Rituals are based on repetition. Repeat something often enough and it becomes a ritual. Finding that one is tiring of any ritual is a hint that the ritual has run its course of value in one's life. The Christ Mind that was in Jesus said, "use not vain repetitions....for they shall not be heard."

Again, rituals are repetitions. They fill a space that never really needed to be filled in the first place. They speak of a higher presence symbolically but don't reveal that Presence—not till a person is exhausted or bored by repetition. At that point the time has come when doing or repeating is over, and God's Presence reveals itself.

Guidance:

Ritualize, if you want, till the personal ego is no more—and God is.

Readiness for Mystical Freedom

The Christ Mind that was in Jesus spoke the words, "And you shall know the Truth—and the Truth shall set you free!" These words have been subject to many scholarly, theological interpretations—but they are truly revealed through mystical awareness. That truth is that there is but one life in the Universe and that everyone and all things are part of this one life—the Creative Universal Presence or God. The truth of being set free mystically refers to being free of the false sense of personal ego identity so that one's soul may experience and benefit from its oneness with Spirit or God.

Understanding this may present a problem:

The problem may be that as you are reading this Mystical Insight, you may already know the mystical description and accept it—but perhaps only on an intellectual level. Knowing and accepting something on an intellectual level is knowing and accepting something by your false personal ego identity—by that illusionary part of yourself that is divided from the whole, the one life, or God. The intellectual acceptance by the personal ego is a ploy or game that this false sense plays to pacify the soul into thinking it is progressing spiritually. If the ploy or game works—then one's spiritual existence goes into limbo. The false personal ego identity may then choose to philosophize with other false personal ego identities about the nature, mysteries, and realities of life but might never get past philosophizing or intellectualizing about reality. One then becomes a scholar of mysticism, but not a mystic. One speaks of the truth, but rarely experiences or lives it except during momentary lapses by the controlling false personal ego.

Knowing the truth intellectually is being in spiritual limbo, while living it is being free.

Now being free is a wonderful state of beingness. It is actually being in contact mystically with Universal Presence or God. It is a sharing of consciousness between the surface part of your awareness and Universal Presence. It is not living out some sort of messianic complex where you feel spiritually superior to others (that would still be part of the personal ego game playing), but instead a full realization that all persons are part of the one Universal consciousness presence—or God. In addition, you do what the Universe guides you to do in helping a few others to join you in mystical awareness and contact—and are patient with the remainder, knowing that, in the illusion of time, their mystical awareness shall come too when God or Universal Presence chooses to awaken them, based upon whether their souls are ready for the reawakening.

Until Universal Presence or God commences the mystical awakening, the personal ego identity lives through another lifetime. As previously alluded to, there may be small fragments of illusionary time where the

Universal Presence inspires or creates, pushing aside the personal ego's control to do so. In such moments of true, spiritually motivated inspiration, the soul is ignited, feeling so moved and so inspired by life. Could one imagine that this is what life would be like if one were free?

Imagine if your mind were to become aware of new insights and new creative ideas on a daily basis, not just on a rare occasion. Imagine being aware of the greater picture of what's really happening—beyond what personal ego comprehension is not seeing because it is too caught up in its illusion of what is taking place. It's a greater life—a greater existence!

It's getting back to and being a part of one's Universal roots, no longer needing to be stimulated by things of this Earth. There is no boredom causing one to run from place to place, although one can still be very active in the illusionary world. But, it is no longer where real activity is experienced. Real activity is experienced in the realm of consciousness. Poets and others who are aware have alluded to the world as being but a stage, a stage where illusionary dramas unfold, whether between people or nations, where the dualistic divide breeds its illusions of love and hate, war and peace, pleasure and pain.

There is a mystical knowing that life Itself is a Universal, eternal process and presence and that earthly, dimensional life is a small part, a small portion of the process—a drop in the ocean of Universal

Consciousness. To be free is to be aware that you are part of such moisture and are part of the ocean's awareness and purpose—or God's Will.

When one is really ready:

Many people say they are easily bored. To cure their immediate sense of boredom they seek some new adventure, be it traveling, doing something new or different, and so on. Now in the physical dimension of this Earth's life, there's nothing wrong with this, for they are edging, slowly, to actually being free. This earthly world is exhausting. The excitement of personal ego adventure eventually becomes exhausted, and the attention is no longer controlled by what is outward but what is inward, so that the eternal stirrings of the soul do awaken.

When one is in companionship with the Universe, one finds that there is no place to go, because in reality, everything is right where you are. There is so much more to experience in the realm of reality than in the illusions of earthly experience. Even the most beautiful scenery on the face of this Earth plane pales when compared to visionary travels in higher realms. The most beautiful things of the Earth are but a hint of the immense beauty that exists in higher realms of Universal Presence.

When individuals are ready, I need not encourage them, for they are already being encouraged and welcomed by Universal Presence within them.

Beyond Thinking

You Are What You Think—or, Thinking Makes It So

Since the advent of what can be described as New Thought Metaphysics, the saying "You are what you think" has been accepted by many. To scores of people it forms the nucleus of positive spirituality. It is the foundation of all positive-thinking movements, whether spiritual or self-help. The concept is that if you think positively, your life will be positive; but the reverse will be true if you think negatively. Carrying this concept still further, entering the psychic realm of interacting energies, there is the so-called law of attraction.

We know that each soul will awaken to certain levels of understanding with every passing lifetime. Souls who are currently in a level of "You are what you think" are basically content that they have achieved some sort of absolute spirituality upon which to base their lives. And, from their previous perspectives of life, they have. There is of course a wide gap between the power of thought metaphysics and the precepts of hell and damnation religion. Therefore, to those who have made this giant leap it would seem that they have possibly arrived at some pinnacle of spiritual wisdom. Plus, from this position emerges still another popular saying: "Your thinking makes it so," which suggests that the power of thought can manifest one's needs or desires.

Factuality and Non-Factuality

Certainly there is truth that if the personal ego level of mind focuses on the positive, other positive, like-minded people will be attracted to that energy. And certainly it is better to have a positive self-image to keep up one's spirits when attempting to accomplish something, even though the positive self-image is associated with one's personal ego identity. Indeed, a person's life will be far better off than having the self-destructive thinking that is so much a part of the hell-and-damnation mindset.

But the true power behind New Thought Metaphysics hasn't been fully grasped by some who think the idea "thinking makes it so" means "Think positively about wealth and prosperity, and wealth and prosperity will be yours." This statement, either directly or indirectly, suggests that one can think one's self—as if one's mind were some kind of mental Aladdin's lamp—into becoming wealthy and prosperous.

We are also told that the power of one's thinking can also keep or make one healthy. By thinking positively about the health of your body—health can be either maintained or restored. In addition, when it comes to life's greatest reward—that of love—the idea is that if you think positively about love, you will attract love.

Now all three premises can help—but they are far from producing the power to make it so.

By thinking positively about wealth and prosperity, you maintain an attitude that serves you well when interacting with other people who could be key figures in having a better material prosperity—but this attitude will not make it so.

By thinking positively about the health of one's body, one certainly can have a better energetic influence over one's body. There's no doubt that, being an energy field made up of energy cells, cellular energy can be influenced by energy factors within the mind. But to think that positive thought will cure or heal what is wrong with oneself is not factual in many cases and conditions. Likewise, to go into denial by affirming that some physical condition does not exist, will not, by such thinking alone, make it go away. It is true, however, that in a large percentage of physical conditions, a condition will clear up on its own—or more specifically, it will clear up through the Presence and Grace of God working in and through the body.

When it comes to creating love in one's life, certainly thinking positively about love produces an outer personal ego sense of identity that makes one more attractive to others and, hence, improves the likelihood that love will come visiting. But, thinking positively about love will not of itself bring love into existence in one's life.

The Reality

In all the life scenarios given as examples above, there is the presence of one common denominator—the false sense of personal ego identity. All such positive thinking takes place within something that is false in and of itself. To generate any real power over anything in one's life that emerges from an illusion is, of itself, an illusion. The best that can be done is to neutralize a small portion of the personal ego's sense of limitation so as to at least suggest that something better or improved is possible. But it will not come as a direct result of positive thinking or that one's thinking makes it so.

So What Is the Reality?

The reality is that only God can make anything so. It is only by the grace of universal power presence that one is prosperous, is healthy or healed, and that one has love or any other thing in life that can be described as a blessing.

The power of universal God Presence is beyond human thinking. It is beyond reason, analysis, logic, and all the other toys found in the toy box of the false sense of personal ego identity. If universal God Presence is the real power behind all human improvement and betterment, both individually and collectively, how do we bring this power for good into our lives?

Think less and be more.

How? Think less every day! Cut down on the amount of so-called time spent on analyzing and picking away at every little detail of your life and the lives of others. If you haven't already, learn to shut down your thought process through meditation. The less you think on the surface level of your mind, the more the possibility that Universal God Consciousness will surface to the frontal part of your consciousness. Eventually thoughts in your mind will be emerging from the universal God Presence within you. Such truly God-Inspired thoughts will provide one with God-Guided Intuitive Thinking. One then experiences Christ-Mindedness such as St. Paul once expressed it: "Let this mind be in you that also was in Christ Jesus."

Other words from the Bible further illustrate the reality spoken of: "as he thinketh in his heart, so is he." Taken to a mystically aware interpretation, these words state that thought originating in the heart, or the place of Universal God Consciousness Presence, is where thought reality really exists. This is consciousness beyond thinking, where thought reality is not simply thought but an awareness of beingness.

Thinking less about what seems to be, letting go to find the Universal God Consciousness Presence within, opens an awareness to beingness where all is known— but not thought about.

Spiritual Healing and Medical Treatment Mystically Viewed

We live in a world of dualities: peace and war, pleasure and pain, wealth and poverty—is it any wonder then that there has been an ongoing conflict between proponents of spiritual and natural healing versus the majority of the medical establishment?

In recent days of this writing of *Mystical Insights,* Dr. Oz, host of the most popular medical show in the United States, has come under attack by some of his medical peers, with some going so far as to accuse him of presenting quackery on his telecasts, albeit he is very respected as a surgeon. In recent years many physicians, like Dr. Oz, have branched out into alternative and complimentary healing modalities as an adjunct to their practice and have had to suffer from their traditional, allopathic peers. So it is not just a matter of conflict between traditional allopathic medicine and those who practice spiritual healing—but also within the ranks of the medical community as well.

Most who are reading this have a metaphysical, transpersonal, or mystical study background and are well aware that spiritual healing has been practiced since the beginnings of recorded time. In the West, the claims of Jesus' healings added an exclamation mark to the practice. Phineas Parkhurst Quimby, who taught Mary Baker Eddy, carried the focus of spiritual health into modern times with the advent of Christian Science. The concept of Christian Science practitioners inspired Ernest Holmes to create Religious Science Practitioners. In between Christian Science and Religious Science, Charles and Myrtle Fillmore placed very heavy emphasis on spiritual healing in the Unity Church movement. And yes, the concept of metaphysical practitioners is part of the International Metaphysical Ministry.

In today's world there are then many forms of spiritual healing approaches being practiced, from the most primitive to the more advanced, with the majority being somewhere in between—whether by traditional Christian fundamentalists, New Age or New Thought movements.

Adding to the dualistic conflict between advocates of spiritual healing and the traditional medical establishment in recent years has been the strong interest by the public in natural healing. Since the idea of natural healing and spiritual healing seem so closely akin, it is very commonplace for those who practice some form of spiritual healing to urge others to more natural lifestyles—to include natural foods, being in nature more often, and so on.

From a higher, mystical viewpoint, excluding the illusion of dualities, health or healing arrived at through what is termed natural healing and spiritual healing are one and the same. In both natural and spiritual healing, the health-maintaining powers and health-restoring powers at work within the body are one and the same. The natural health practitioner may describe this inner power as the body's natural healing and health presence to heal itself—while those involved in spiritual healing (minus so many spiritual egos involved in spiritual healing) will attribute good health or health restoration to God's Power working in the body. From a mystical view, as previously explained, they are one and the same.

Yes, a very small percentage of allopathic medical doctors acknowledge the spiritual and natural methodologies to health maintenance and restoration, but unfortunately those are still a small minority. At the same time, there are likewise extremists carrying the spiritual and natural banners into war against established medical practice, which they see as big business and big pharmaceutical companies favoring profits over human health concerns. Add to this the fancy footwork of insurance companies and governmental health interventions, and the spiritual and natural health practitioners have a lot to point a finger at. But should we not be remiss: let's not forget the chemically altered food industry that has high financial stakes in producing more food. But at what cost, one might ask, to the health of the body? The father of medicine, Hippocrates, once stated, "Food is the best medicine." It is left to you to answer, would he say the same about much of today's chemically altered food?

And so in this world of illusionary dualities, the wars and conflicts between spiritual healing and medical treatment wages on.

With mystical awareness, there should be no conflict, because conflict is an illusion of egos caused by false personal ego identities of most of the spiritual/natural healers on one hand and the traditional allopathic medical doctors on the other. Mystically speaking, both are playing out their roles of feeding their false personal ego identities. The two should be as one, demonstrating the One Universal Life Presence of God manifesting through them for the good of those seeking to preserve their good health and those seeking to restore it.

In a world, dimension, planet or whatever the habitat where the oneness of life is recognized, those of the spiritual/natural healing professions and the medical profession would be under one roof. All factors of beingness—body, mind, and soul—each would now be treated by a holistic approach for the whole person. We would no longer have a war of methodologies based on the limited awareness of personal egos, but rather we would have peace and understanding, all working for the good of the person seeking preventative care or healing.

If one wishes to criticize the medical profession with all its technical advancements, there is much—so very much—to criticize. Yet, it is to be very praised for the advancements it has made in preventative care and treatment. At the same time, if criticism is directed toward spiritual/natural practitioners, here too, there is an abundance to be critical of, for without mystical awareness and guidance, the greater majority operate out of false personal ego identities—not a good atmosphere for actual spiritual/natural healing—or more specifically, for God's Power to be actively present.

Mystical Reality

Not everyone on the physical Earth plane of existence will be healed, whether through spiritual/natural or medical means. A goodly percentage will pass on to the afterlife, and some will continue to be here even though discomfort and pain will be present. Whether you believe this to be as a result of bad karma, or to teach the healthy how very important health is and to avoid the mistakes they made is left to you to decide.

Those whose good health is maintained, together with those whose health is restored, may give credit and thanks to their spiritual/natural practitioner or their medical physician. And those who are aware and have received both restoration of health and maintained good health—may give credit to both. But, mystically speaking, the credit really goes to the one life universal God Presence living in everyone, by whose grace, good health, and wellness do prevail or have been restored.

The scalpel in the hands of the surgeon is directed by God's Presence, and the very same inner God

Presence guides the spiritual/natural practitioner's methods.

In a perfect world of beingness, issues of health are nonexistent. Only pure beingness is. No dualities, no conflicts—just being. There is nothing to seek that is called health and nothing to avoid that is called sickness. All are one—all are simply peaceful beingness. Duality and personal ego identity are no longer even a memory; for memory is thought, and beingness is without thought—only a blissful beingness, ultimate oneness, love in the absolute. In such a state of beingness, all that once was in need of healing has long since been healed. Measured time and its illusion have been replaced with the reality of one eternal moment of Universal beingness.

Whether spiritual, medical, or in the forward merger of both, be it for preventative care or wellness restoration, reread the preceding paragraph daily for yourself and those you care for.

In the mystical reality of God's Oneness—all is already resolved as wholeness. And—so it is.

Spiritual Power— Illusions and Reality

Healing, magic, mind over matter, invoking the gods or God—all are, have been, and will be a part of the human species' quest to have spiritual power work for themselves or others. Since the beginning of recorded time on this physical Earth plane of existence, human beings have reached for a higher spiritual power to work on their behalf or for others. However, many have noticed that sometimes a higher power seems to work and other times it does not. Is one person using the right prayer or incantation while another is not?

Why does invoking spiritual power seem so inconsistent in the hands of humankind? Why is it that not all prayers are answered for health, healing, prosperity, love, and other human needs and desires? Are some prayers chosen or favored while others are not? Is it a matter of good or bad karma, the wrong religion, or the wrong slant on God or spirituality?

Candidly, no one has any extra or special spiritual power going for them, despite what they might imagine from their false sense of personal ego identity. Spiritual power that is active in one's life is available only when the personal ego is not trying to influence it.

In human reality, all may seem possible in regard to spiritual power as harnessed or brought about through many diverse forms of spiritual practice. Now, it's true that many prayers or other spiritual practices seem to be answered—but they only seem to be answered. Of course, it is recognized that these words do not meet with a favorable response from those who believe that humans have the personal ego means to bring about some form of divine interventional power. Certainly it will seem that, in the lives of many, God or some other spiritual power has answered them. And yes—it seems that way.

In reality, human consciousness, as it is currently awakened collectively in the mass of humanity, is not capable of influencing spiritual power. If it were, the entirety of the Universe would be one gigantic cosmic mess—one explosion after another as human beings in their present states of consciousness attempted to influence and find balance within the energy forces of nature on a universal scale. Place real spiritual power in the hands of a fool, that is, one with a limited perception of what really is at work on a universal scale, and chaos would ensue.

Those who are at a deep level of spiritual slumber—though they seem awake—may be led to believe that even if they themselves can't invoke spiritual power, there are those who can. And certainly there are those who are lined up and ready to fulfill the fantasy, either for their own personal good or in some way to satisfy their own self-delusions of spiritual power at their disposal.

Albert Schweitzer once made this comment about healing in the practice of medicine: "The role of the physician is to amuse the patient long enough so as to allow nature time to do the actual healing." Now certainly, most metaphysically, mystically, or esoterically inclined people would agree with Schweitzer's statement suggesting that ultimately it is nature that does the bottom-line healing.

The very same principle could apply to the seeming use of spiritual power in any practice of spiritual healing. One could paraphrase Schweitzer with these words: The role of the spiritual healer is to give hope to the person in need of healing until God actually does the healing—be it instantaneous or over a period of seeming time. That's if a healing is to take place, whether through medical or spiritual practice. Medical physicians do lose patients—and ministries lose parishioners. In both instances, it is up to a higher power to decide who continues to live in the physical dimension—or whose time it is to move on to an after physical life plane of existence. But, nothing in nature is ever lost—it just continues in another energy rate of existence.

The same understanding can be applied to all other practices attempting to bring spiritual power into play, whether it be wealth building, love, power, human fame, or glory. All is an attempt of the imaginary personal ego's attempt to influence energies greater than human power. If one's personal ego seems to succeed, it can further delude itself into thinking it has really done something spiritually to activate spiritual power in his or her own life or in the life of another. This assumption can further add to the egotism of the false personal ego identity.

Now, stop in your tracks for a mental moment and hear the mystical reality of the words coming forth from the Christ Mind that was in Jesus:

"Why call me good? It is not I but the Father (God) that doeth these good works." These are words of reality from a presence to whom many would attribute the greatest healings and miracles. Does any labeled spiritual healer, magician, or caster of spells claim to have greater spiritual power than was claimed for the Christ in Jesus? If so—appear to me now, and I will be silent. If not, it is time for one's own self-styled form of spiritual importance to still itself.

Only God's Power is real. And, in a Godly self-aware Universe, It knows what needs to be manifested, by whom and when, and whether on an infinite or finite scale. What then can be done for those wishing to manifest God's Will? Grow in awakening in consciousness to God's Presence within yourself. The more awakened you become, the more you'll realize that a human being alone and at this present level of awakening cannot control or invoke spiritual power.

Again, what you can do of yourself (personal ego identity) to influence spiritual power—is nothing.

There's an old song whose lyrics go, "Whatever will be, will be." Add to it the words, "for it already is." So—relax—and let God's Will be done, as it will be anyway. Go with the Biblical words, "not my will, but Thy will be done." If you are a spiritual healer or some form of spiritual practitioner—go through the motions and do your work. But as you do, constantly remind the recipient and yourself, that if improvement comes about, the personal you had nothing to do with it and that a healing or manifestation came about as a result of the will, grace, and the power of God.

Keep in mind, be it yours or a recipient's, that life is an ongoing process of seemingly different stages, and that in the final analysis, God's Will is for the ultimate good of every soul. The worst of the worst is not permanent—but a prelude to the best of the best.

All that has been discussed here is included in the words so commonly spoken in metaphysical spirituality: "Let Go, and Let God." For, until we do not sit at the right hand of God—but are the right hand of God—real spiritual power is God's alone.

And, in the human mind's meanderings, let all be glad that it is so—and so it is!

Prostitution—Realistically and Mystically Viewed

The urge and the power to create—so powerful that the unmanifest moved within Itself to create manifestation. And because all that was manifested was of the very same presence, the power to create was similarly powerful within the creations. The infinite power to create remains one with its finite creation—the human being. Male and female energies of duality, instinctively moved by sexuality, a power greater than themselves, instinctively feel the pull to be joined with each other sexually.

What has all of this to do with prostitution? To the point—everything. To understand the presence of prostitution, one must understand it mystically—meaning the driving power to act sexually. The power of universal creation process is behind every human urge toward sexual activity. To prove the point, one has only to look at some of the misfortunes of some famous modern men in high positions whose urge toward sexuality overcame them, driving them to risk everything that it might have taken them years to build, now lost to the sexual push within them. They gambled their positions to satisfy this powerful drive, and presidents, kings, politicians, and clergy have succumbed.

Such is the power—the relentless driving for sexual contact. It should be no wonder, then, that the world's oldest profession came to be and still exists. This dualistic society, made up of masculine and feminine energy, is powered by a Universal Presence in the physiological chemistry of both men and women. In such an environment, prostitution has always found its place—and always will. Can anyone deny that there is a need for sexual activity in this dualistic earthly dimension? Can this power be repressed? Far too many of the clergy have proven that this power cannot be repressed or restrained. The power to act sexually is just too powerful in humanity.

But we cannot forget that there are places in today's so-called modern world where women are still stoned to death for sexual acts unacceptable to primitive understandings of life. Yes, such hypocrisy is still with us long after the words uttered by the Christ Mind of Jesus: "he that is without sin among you, let him first cast the stone."

In such an atmosphere on this planet, in this earthly dimension, prostitution flourishes. The question is, should it? After all, critics would argue that it debases women. And, would that not also apply to the customer—debasing men as well? Candidly, the only ones debased are those who attack it openly but hypocritically engage in it behind closed doors. Begin to pierce the veils of decency in any society and the basic premise of prostitution is very much present. How many people today, for example, are married—both women and men—but are joined for financial or material reasons?

In commenting about this last example—especially for a mystical understanding—the preceding remarks have not been made just to be critical, but only to view what could be called prostitution in a larger perspective. An even larger perspective is that the unrelenting Power toward sexual activity is everywhere so much a part of the human being—be it in the subtle maneuverings of a seducer or in the gross, harmful expressions of a sexual assault.

Prostitution is acknowledging life as it really is on the earthly physical dimension, not as its critics would wish it to be. But, does prostitution have a legitimate place in society?

Those who gladly and willingly, without coercion of any kind, engage in prostitution are, in their own way, knowingly or unknowingly, a part of spirituality expressed in physical form as union. For the sexually disadvantaged, it may be as close as they may ever get to at least some semblance of human warmth, which is God's Presence surfacing—even if it is but just for a brief moment.

In the United States there is currently great emphasis being placed on the coming home of veterans who have been disabled by serving in the military. Shall such young men, still with the powerful libido of youth, be told that, due to their disability, normal relationships leading to sexuality be forsaken for the remainder of their lives? Similarly, shall many who are socially challenged be told that they should forgo sexuality? And, shall those who have dedicated their life to the caring of an aged relative or others and cannot find the time to find someone with whom to have sexual relations in their lives, be denied? The answers to those questions are left to you.

If prostitution could answer the call of so many—why has it been so shunned? The stock answer is—it's degrading. It is degrading when one is forced to be active through dire financial need where nothing else seems to be an alternative—or when one is forced into prostitution and held in it by another. Force takes away from the freedom of the soul and is an affront to universal freedom manifesting in human form.

Sexuality emanating from free will is only sinful or an error when its presence takes precedent over the importance of God in one's life. When universal God Presence dominates a person's consciousness, sexuality, and the driving power behind it, is seen as a natural activity of the creative process powered by the Universal Creative Presence of God.

What is described as sexuality in fact exists in many dimensions of the Universe—from far more barbaric expressions among dimensions spiritually lower than the physical dimension and in far, far higher expressions in highly spiritual dimensions of being where energy exchange is the most natural experience of union as unconditional love, or God's Love, expressed. Such dimensions are the final level of union before ultimate union or absorption into God Beingness.

Human sexuality seen for what it really is—is a stepping stone to eventual reuniting with or union with God. God bless those who willingly serve the needs of others—in whatever capacity.

The Illusionary Perception of Time and Space

With each discovery in astronomy, there is often an awestruck wonderment about the vastness of space. As science gives greater analysis to such cosmological findings, common knowledge of the age and immensity of the universe grows. Humanity is caught up in expanding perceptions of time and space. No longer are such perceptions confined to scientists and professors; the human mind staggers as mass media communicates through videos how enormous are the reaches in time and light years between the physical dimension of Earth and the manifestations of the cosmos.

And yet—mystically, is there more at work here in the perception of time and space?

Mystical awareness removes the veils of what seems to be and what really is. And truth comes to the forefront when it comes to the mind's perception of time and space.

The stunning reality is that both time and space are illusionary perceptions as perceived in human awareness.

Human sense perception is confined to certain boundaries—held captive by a limited awareness. All frames of reference concerning time and space are, in fact, held in check by human awareness. Furthermore, all scientific discoveries can only be understood within the parameters of this awareness. There are reasons for this, which is why creation or manifestation exists.

The illusions of time and space are necessary components of manifestation and creation. Such illusions include the dualities of beginnings and endings, the seeming occurrences of human birth and death as well as the birth and death of a star—from human to the cosmos—beginnings and endings and the seeming time in between. In mystical awareness there is but one life in this Universe and as this Universe, including all of its various dimensions—manifesting as everything and everyone. An illusion of separateness and variety exists in order to make the illusion seem very real. The one life, Universal Consciousness has created a cosmic illusion to create diversification of Itself.

Only the one life Presence of God exists as, and within, all, creating and maintaining thought-form images and the environmental illusion of both time and space to substantiate existence as it appears to our senses to be. Again, all present scientific discoveries—or those in the future—are still constrained by the illusion of what life seems to be.

Dualities, diversities, beginnings, and endings are all part of the cosmic drama. They make creation work. They provide the illusion of time and space. Yet, the one life remains a constant, without beginning or ending and without the illusion of travel, moving from point A to point B, or the time needed in between that journey to make it appear that travel and elapsed time have taken place.

Yes, it all seems very real, and each new discovery of science captures the human mind into justifying beliefs that time and space do exist. Yet, the ultimate reality of one life, Universal Life, or God—is the only realty that exists. From the Bible are the words, "In the beginning God created the heaven and the Earth . . . And God said 'Let there be light,' and there was light." And from light all things came forth. Human beings, other beings, the cosmos, the perception of time—all are seeming divisions within the light, the seeming first manifestation of God or unmanifest spirit.

Only eternity—one cosmic second—actually exists, and that description is only given to fill a human need for a point of reference as to describing eternity as timelessness.

Again, why is the illusion necessary? Because without it God could not create what to human awareness appears to be a created universe with a seeming enormity of manifesting life forms residing throughout the physical as well as other dimensions.

In a higher state of beingness, life or existence is more known for what it is and why it is. The value of the eternal or God, Creator Presence replaces what human consciousness values; fragmentary perceptions of one's life are replaced with a holistic awareness of life and the Universe. The need for personal ego existence is seen as a constricting handicap to reality. With a greater awareness of reality comes an enhanced appreciation of all manifested life. With the diminishing of the personal ego, which is the source of all human problems, there is an increasing awareness that one is a part of the eternal whole rather than a mere, fragmentary, isolated, ego.

In such an expanded awareness of reality and existence there is a greater opportunity for expression, as human awareness is increasingly free of seeming limitations. Consciousness is freer to explore and express itself in creative and unique ways. The more one's consciousness opens to the truth of the only one consciousness of God, the more consciousness within any seeming creation is freed to be.

The soul's purpose for this incarnation becomes increasingly evident. Plus, it is a mystical truth that only when the soul's purpose is fulfilled in any incarnation that lasting fulfillment and happiness can be achieved. In a state of awareness free of the illusion of time and space, we are freer to be what we are really—an individualized expression of the one life, Universal Presence of God—expressing a unique attribute of itself through its creation within itself and of itself.

One should have an awareness that all that could be—already is the one Universal Life Presence of God, and we live in the eternal Consciousness of God. We have not come from somewhere—for in truth we have never left. There is no place to get to that requires the illusion of time and space—for again, we have never left. All that could be—already is the one Universal Life Presence of God.

These mystically aware words from the Bible highlight reality: "For in Him (God) we move, and live, and have our being." Add to this truth the mystical message from the Mind of Christ in Jesus: "I am Alpha and Omega [true God Selfhood], the beginning and the ending...."

Life is not what we make it—but ultimately what we awaken to find it already is.

War and Peace— Beyond This World?

All truth is contained in the consciousness of all human beings. The ultimate state of consciousness or beingness, which is God's Presence, is deeply imbedded in everyone's unconsciousness. Within the deeper memory levels of the mind are memories of the past as well as memories of the future, which, despite the illusion of time have already happened.

Whatever has been—is. Whatever will be—already is. Within the mind or consciousness contained within every human being is a doorway into the past and entrance to the future, each of which already is.

The mind in fact contains many doorways or entrances into various levels of existence and, in fact, into other worlds. During inner activity of the mind seeking God, a person may come into direct contact with a large variety of contacts. Such contacts, for the most part, are with other dimensions of existence and, on lesser occasions, with the earthly dimension in the physical plane of outer space.

One who has achieved mystical awareness can even see and/or know certain realities which to outer human sense perception would usually be classified by clinicians in today's world as a mental or psychotic experience.

However, what a clinical psychologist or psychiatrist of today might classify as a psychotic experience may be, to one of mystical awareness, a higher reality. It is no wonder, then, that at some time, in a relaxed ego state, an experience may surface from the deeper levels of the unconscious into the surface level to reveal activities beyond this Earth—be it in the physical dimension or other realms as well.

With such glimpses into other worlds and their activities, the mystically aware mind becomes knowledgeable about what takes place beyond this earthly and dimensional existence of Earth. The physical universe is vast and other dimensions also offer a variety of existences. Many parts of the physical universe and other dimensions are inhabited—from existences that are less aware than those on the physical/Earth dimension to the highest ethereal forms of beingness.

Excluding the very highest dimensions of existence (just a hairline beneath the existence of Universal Consciousness or God), there exists a vast array of beings living their lives in varying forms and environments. Some are similar to appearances on the physical Earth and others could only be said to be— very unique in their appearance. Imagine for a moment what exotic or strange life forms one might encounter if one were to travel to the depths of oceans on this planet (which certainly has been proven by deep oceanic photography). If such strange life forms can exist on this planet in this dimension, does it not then make common sense that life forms beyond what the human level of the mind could conceive—do exist.

We live in an absolutely incredible consciousness or universal God Mind reality. Yet, in spite of all the tremendous variety of all life forms, human existence can find commonality, even though there is the illusion of separateness or seeming dualities. Pleasure, pain, birth, death—all of the dualities present in the physical Earth plane are also existent in other planes of existence as well as the physical plane throughout the cosmos. Why must duality, of necessity, exist? So we may have the illusion of seeming existence apart from the one universal life of God.

Yes, where there is duality, there is also the breeding ground or environment conducive to conflict, conflict between individual life forms and collective groupings of life forms.

In this world what one hears about in the expression "the war between forces of light and darkness" does exist throughout a very high percentage of the Universe.

The great psychologist, Carl Jung, once said that within mythology there is hidden truth. Those mythological stories that have been accepted by many as only myth—the stories of wars even between the Gods or more awakened beings—may, in fact, have emerged from the myth creators' unconscious realities to the surface of their minds. These myths hold the truth that where there is variety, diversity—and duality—there is the environment for conflict, whether from an altercation between individual life forms or collective groupings in conflict or war.

So, is there peace anywhere in this Universe, in either seen or in unseen dimensions? Yes and no. As in this physical Earth dimension, there is a season for all things—a time for war and a time for peace—except for those life forms just beneath the Universal Consciousness of God. Those life forms can be described, for the sake of some human form of reference, as Christ or light beings—God's first dimension of beingness apart from Spirit. Here—there is peace, for all know themselves as one, with no illusion of duality leading to conflict and war—just one universal life simultaneously existing in forms barely distinguishable from the light in which they reside and are.

Here on this physical Earth plane there never will be permanent peace, only passing seasons—a dualistic existence of times for war and times for peace. If some feel an urging from within to seek peace—let them seek it within themselves by drawing closer to that urge, which is God's eternal peace calling one to its presence.

There is an idea expressed in Hindu scripture that proclaims that even the Gods on their high thrones in Heaven envy those on Earth, for humans can travel [through meditation] beyond the Gods to the ultimate God of all. In such an inner journey the human soul can rise above dimensions, even those dimensions of the Gods (that may even be in a time of conflict) to that state of God Beingness that the Bible describes as "the Peace which passeth all understanding." Only through finding and becoming united with the collective universal soul, the Paramatman, or the Christ Presence within oneself can the eternal presence and peace be found.

Remember that God's peace is closer to you than your next breath—and is present between your thoughts.

Today's Clinical Psychology and Psychiatry in Contrast with an Enlightened Society

Except for a few souls in this world who are mystically aware, the practice of psychology and psychiatry will not create a truly mentally healthy society. As it currently stands, the world standard for mental health is collective neurosis. The occupation of the clinical psychologist and psychiatrist is to adjust the mind to be functional in a dysfunctional society. What is called mental health is the ability to function with that which is dysfunctional collectively. The illusions of one's personal isolation must be made to fit into the illusions and vogue of whatever is considered reality in present-day society.

The basis of identity as viewed by clinical psychology and psychiatry is that the self, one's identity, is that of a personal ego identity, a product of an organism bumping up against its environment through a long period of time—first to form a simple awareness of itself and eventually to evolve into an environmentally created identity or ego. Put enough egos together and you form an ego society. If, for whatever reason, one ego cannot function within the collective ego society in which it dwells, it then is considered dysfunctional, with the role of today's mental health clinician being to adjust it, to get it back into step with the collective thinking, the neurosis of today's ego society.

The flaw in all this is that a society comprised of personal ego identities is still a society of persons isolated from each other by virtue of believing themselves to be separate, isolated entities. And, separate, personal egos are fragile at best. They can be quickly shattered in moments by an outward life-changing event. When individuals do find common ground together or when groups rally around some common belief of heritage or ideology, this fragmentary sense of separateness can seem diminished. This sense of belonging, of meaning can seem to flourish under the banner of religious, nationalistic, or lifestyle beliefs. Each, in its own way, encourages the illusion of meaning in personal ego existence collectively.

But in truth these personal egos still have no foundation, no reality in truth or in fact. They are not seen as part of an eternal whole, but rather as fragments of an illusionary existence. When identity is viewed as a personal ego identity, even if it functions within its societal group—it is still an isolated entity unto itself. And, being still an isolated ego identity, it can function within the collective group for a time until, given the right (or wrong) set of circumstances, it finds itself in conflict with others or with the collective group.

Of course clinical psychology and psychiatry will defend itself by stating that it is not in the business of philosophy or religion: It is in the business of making people functional within the collective framework of society. As clinical psychology and psychiatry currently stand—that is a true assessment. The problem is that they become the spokespersons or standard bearers for what society is to believe about the mind and—most importantly—human identity. In this manner the illusion of personal ego identity is perpetuated, continuing the ego-centered, fragmented society that breeds conflict and wars.

In contrast, in an enlightened society occupied by enlightened souls, clinical psychology and psychiatry as they are currently practiced would—at best—be considered primitive. Why? In an enlightened society, personal ego identity would not exist. The mind would be considered a channel through which universal consciousness could be expressed. All members of an enlightened society would know themselves to be individualized expressions of some unique attributes of the Universal whole, Universal Presence/Mind/Spirit—or God.

Souls incarnating into such a society would not have to be taught about the relationship to the Universal Whole or Presence, for they would incarnate with a knowingness of their reality. They would incarnate not to serve temporary rules, but to be consciously co-creative with Universal Presence. For these reasons, in such an enlightened society of soul minds, clinical psychology or psychiatry would not exist. Religion, as it is now known on the physical Earth plane, would not exist. They would not exist because, from whatever frame of reference one would choose to think about an enlightened society, such a society would be a collection of Christs, Buddhas, Krishnas, and so on. The common denominator for all persons would be universal consciousness identity—created forms embodying one universal mind.

What Is the Bottom Line?

There is no doubt that clinical psychology and psychiatry do play a major role in society by attempting to care for those who are severely mentally ill, and they should be thanked and acknowledged for their efforts. This commentary is directed toward working with people who are not suffering from some psychosis, but rather from psychoneurosis. With this in mind, let's go on to what can be done.

We must keep in mind though that, with but few exceptions, those who enter the field of clinical psychology and psychiatry are basically illusionary personal egos attempting to treat other illusionary personal egos so that they may function within an illusionary society comprised of illusionary, inwardly fragmented, fragile, personal, ego-centered identities.

Such a society is a virtual breeding ground for conflicts and further isolation in the future—until an egotistically driven maniac collects groupings of people, unhappy and unfulfilled by their existence, and directs them into another war, feeding them with the illusion that such conquest will fill the void within their souls. Such has been, and will ever be, the repeating history of this physical Earth plane.

To be of value, clinical psychology and psychiatry should have two objectives:

The first is to do what they have been doing, which is to make a person functional within the neurotic whole. This would then serve to facilitate communication for the important second objective.

The second objective would be to lay the seeds for a new concept of identity—universal identity with oneness. To be certain, for the vast majority of persons, universal identity, oneness with God, would be but a concept, and they would not be suddenly transformed into enlightened mystics. But, the seeds would have been planted to grow in the soil of future lifetimes.

To meet the needs of those who are functional in a collective ego-based society and who feel an inner God Presence prompting them to move beyond a personal ego-based psychological understanding of the mind and consciousness, the International Metaphysical Ministry founded the Theocentric Life Society.

This specialized ministry utilizes educational counseling and life coaching in Theocentric Psychology. Theocentric Psychology's focus is on completing the understanding of the mind and consciousness, emphasizing that consciousness comes from one creative source, namely Universal Mind/Spirit/God, and that true identity is being aware of oneness and the cooperation of the outer human with the inner Spirit. In this way, the soul is freed of the collective neurosis that binds it, bringing forth universal consciousness and its God-provided potentials.

The universal process has been served.

The universal embryo has been nourished.

Why Life?
The Purpose of it All

What's the meaning, the purpose to it all?

With the exception of philosophers, theologians, and a few deep thinkers, most people live their lives without questioning—why? Why does tend to surface in most people's lives, be it ever so briefly, at the time of some life-changing event which greatly impacts their emotions, such as a transition (death), a painful or crippling illness or accident, the tragedies of war, and similar experiences which shake the foundations of an otherwise structured life.

When things are going right, a person gets caught up in the positive quality of life and feels no need to question. On the other hand, when things go painfully wrong, a person questions. If life contains so many experiences that are filled with pain and sorrow—why live at all?

Beautiful moments are times to experience life without question—while painful ones invoke the question—why? Why can't life simply be all pleasure—just an endless series of blessings? Why all the misery in the world? Are moments of misery necessary to better appreciate the good?

So very many have tried to answer such questions so as to bring meaning and purpose to their own lives. Is a higher reality attempting to teach its creations certain lessons, or, as some have speculated, is God, Universal Mind testing their spiritual resolve or commitment?

When God creates a human being, God has seemingly individualized into a form. And this form—or more specifically, a thought form within the mind of God—can seem to fall away from oneness with the God Mind. It seems to have formed what it believes to be an individual, separate and apart from its Creator. But in truth, it has never left the Mind of God in which it was created and resides.

The moment separateness takes over the consciousness of the human thought form in the Mind of God is the moment that separateness—false personal ego identity—takes over the form. Then, separateness and duality rule the mind. Duality breeds contrasts: heat and cold, pleasure and pain, war and peace, wellness and sickness, love or loneliness. What eventually follows is the human/Earth dimension of consciousness, where ultimate one life/God reality is substituted with an illusion of living human/Earth dimensional life.

But why?

For a moment imagine a vast consciousness— Universal Mind/Spirit/God, that is inactive. It knows its own existence, and it is inactive and simply—is. It is allness, a oneness or union of all; and in that allness of union there is love—the full beingness of love as a result of absolute union.

There is a cosmic stillness, a beingness of love unexpressed.

Imagine now this state of love, which simply is, but is unexpressed. For if all is absolute union or love, then who or what can it express that to? God/love/absolute union is alone. Though it is everything, it is still alone. To express, therefore, God/love must create. Yet it cannot create anything apart from itself, for it is All. Therefore, God or love creates an illusion of something that appears to be separate—but in truth is not.

First, the manifestation or light is manifested within the unmanifested. The light gives the illusion of dividing itself. All the divisions of light give a further illusion of individual entities. Yet, because the light is so active in these entities, they still know that they are part of God, living in reality within God as God lives within them— they are individualized expressions of God's beingness of love or absolute union.

Expression, at last: Such expressions form what can be described as the *highest angelic realm*. God expresses love to them and through them, while they express love back to God. God loves and is loved in return. In this flow of love God is acknowledged: God Presence can rightly declare to its creations—"I am that I am."

However, because of the illusion of separateness, dualistic concepts of time and space begin to occupy the consciousness of the angelic entities. Consciousness begins to yield to an illusion of divisions. Over a period of illusionary time, the divisions cause a dimming of the angelic Oneness with God, even though, in truth, they have never left God's Presence. In truth they are God's Presence.

But some within the angelic realm begin to believe they are separate entities apart from God. The personal ego begins to cloud these consciousnesses. Illusion continues until they can no longer exist in dimensional consciousness just a light step away from allness or God.

They become "fallen angels."

As the illusion of time continues, energy factors continue to change until forms of physical energy/matter and a corresponding landscape dimension develop. Some of the fallen angelic do not fall all the way into the physical dimensions. Some retain enough of their oneness with God to occupy higher energy realms or the dimensions of the Gods.

The Universal/Eternal Bottom Line?

Keep the divine remembrance. Maintain a remembrance or an awareness that all that has been described is still simply an illusion, one illusion giving birth to other illusions. In truth, stripped away of all illusions, only the one Universal Life Mind/Spirit—God—exists.

So why life, at least life as mortals comprehend it? So that God, allness, total union as total love may express love. To express, God must create. And, being all, it must create within itself. God as love can express love to and through its creations—and in turn be loved or acknowledged as presence.

Life/creation is eternal love—or God expressed.

This is the meaning and purpose of life.

If one dissolves all illusions of separateness from God/Universal Allness, this purpose or meaning to life is what will be found; or in the mystical meaning of the words from the Bible, "above all these things, is love."

Choice Reality

As you go through life living every day, always realize that life exists on many levels. What we see and perceive to be real on an outer physical level is but the outer shadow of a far greater reality at work. This applies to both the outer appearance of good as well as that which, when carried to an extreme, one perceives to be evil. Both heaven and hell exist in the human psyche. The spiritually aware person is aware of the dualistic warfare taking place within and needs to make a choice. Either the personal ego is in charge, which leans the mind and soul towards the dark side, or the personal ego is set aside in favor of the light of God's indwelling reality.

If the truth be truly known, it is not a matter of personal choice as most people of any faith believe; instead the choice is God's. When a soul has reached a point in reawakening to God's Presence, it is God that makes the choice. The personal ego has nothing to do with it, for the personal ego would do everything it could to retain power.

So what is the point to all just said?

The point is that all is done for us by the grace or love of God, for we are God's manifestations.

Be well, be aware, and be an acknowledgement that your life exists by the grace that is God's Love for you, Spirit's creation.

Guruism

The only true teacher or guru is to be found within oneself.

There's an old Hindu expression that goes, "when the *chela* (student) is ready, the guru (teacher) will appear." Until a soul has spiritually awakened satisfactorily to a higher awareness, it continues to look outward to find a guru or spiritual teacher to provide a passage from mortal to immortal consciousness.

A true teacher will shun grandiose, spiritual accolades and simply be a spiritual signpost – pointing students back into themselves.

Such information may contradict the adoration by many students for those who might be described as being from the spiritual bloodline of gurus bestowing enlightenment on those who seek it. That adoration, however, is still one more illusion that even the most earnest may encounter.

True spiritual teachers know that only the all-knowing within oneself can provide ultimate enlightenment. Only Universal Consciousness, Mind,

Spirit, or God within oneself can provide the ultimate spiritual experience.

When students are moved by the greater within themselves – and are truly ready to be true teachers or gurus themselves, then the real inner teacher will provide them all that is needed.

The point is – listen only to teachers who say to you, "Listen only to the still small voice within yourself that is the sound of Universal Presence." Realize that all else they may speak of, while interesting, is superfluous to the real goal of life – connecting in mystical union with the ultimate teacher within yourself.

Be within while accomplishing without, knowing that you need not seek truth outwardly – for when you are ready truth will seek you from within.

Moving from Temporal to Eternal

When one contemplates eternity, it brings a sense of something that is timeless, without beginning or ending—something that has always been and will always be. Let's step forward in concept and realize that all— you, me, and everyone—exist in and as a part of eternity. In this earthly plane we exist in time and we are part of humanness—but in absolute reality, we are existent within and as a part of eternity.

Now eternity and all that it is, has always existed and thus has had sufficient endless time to become conscious of itself. All timed existences, inclusive of humanity, are as thought processes moving within eternity. Eternity or eternal life is another way of describing the ultimate life consciousness of all that is, or—God.

When one surrenders his or her personal ego and will to God and God's Will, one is in fact surrendering to eternity or eternal life presence.

Foreverness then begins with any human who realizes that eternal value of surrendering the temporary illusion of a personal ego to eternity or God's Presence within him or herself.

The soul is then in union or synthesis with Spirit and lives on as part of eternal presence.

Earthly Incarnation

Everyone—every soul—incarnates on this Earth plane because they belong to a certain level of consciousness or awareness, except for a very few souls who are in a higher state of awareness. These few higher souls are here to raise those souls' awarenesses that are ready to be raised. The readiness is not brought about by any religion or spiritual teacher—but from God's Presence within a soul that knows a soul is now aware sufficiently to awaken to more of reality.

The vast majority of souls who are not awakened are drawn to incarnate on this Earth plane of existence. This Earth plane is a plane of contrasts—day or night, heat or cold, love or loneliness, health or illness, wealth or poverty, pleasure or pain, war or peace. The vast majority of souls incarnate into the Earth plane of contrasts and contradictions because their state of consciousness or soul state is filled with contrasts or contradictions.

Pleasure and pain, war or peace, are extremes. If one lives in extremes as one's reality, then the return upon return to this Earth plane is inevitable. We can only live in an environment that reflects what we are.

Only in oneness can the cycle of birth and rebirth be brought to an end. Only in oneness within oneself, where the extremes of contrasts, contradictions, and conflicts have been outgrown, can a soul be in a higher existence than the Earth plane.

An awakening soul becomes increasingly aware that living in extremes must be set aside to awaken a greater reality, a reality of oneness with Universal God/Mind/Spirit Consciousness that exists as the essence of peace. In such an awakening, future incarnations or manifestations will be in existences of peace.

The Silence of Absolute Love

The Christ Mind that was in Jesus expressed life's goal in these words: "And now abide faith, hope, and love, these three; but the greatest of these is love."

Beyond human definitions of silence and love, there exists the realm of original silence, peace, and love, where conflict and duality do not exist and where all are in ultimate union with the one. Here, no words need be spoken or thoughts responded to. Being in absolute love is to open oneself to absolute silence, peace, presence, or God.

In a world dominated with practical necessities, there can be nothing more practical than having a consciousness able to find an absolute silent clarity of mind—so at peace that it can see through worldly confusion and duality to know what is truly necessary in this world.

This same state of silent clarity is one with absolute love, peace, and presence. This means that all practicalities, dualities, and conflicts can be, or are to be, met with a greeting of absolute love, not just for the good of one individual situation or one soul, but for the greater good of all beings—who are, in truth, one with All.

Attaining such a state of silence and loving presence provides all that is necessary to live in this earthly world and in worlds beyond—in loving silence, peace, and pure presence, where words are not necessary.

Multi-Dimensional Universes

While physical science is moving increasingly to an acceptance of multi-physical universes, mystics, who have long since known this, are aware of an even greater complexity—specifically, the existence of numerous nonphysical dimensions within each physical dimension.

Expanding this multi-dimensional reality from a collective one of universes to each individual's human reality, there comes a realization that every soul on life's eternal path exists in different dimensions simultaneously. This expansion of inner awareness brings realization that the soul, or true Self, exists simultaneously in many dimensions and in several different expressions of beingness.

When the psalmist uttered the words, "You are fearfully and wonderfully made," it was quite likely spoken with an awareness of how vast even one human existence is in its multiplicity.

Likewise, when the Christ Mind that was in Jesus spoke the words, "I am in this world, but not of it," the words conveyed an awareness of the multiple layers of what truly constitutes the reality of the self.

As a person goes through the earthly plane's dimensional life, may there always be an awareness that there is far more to life than the physical senses can perceive and that the wisest action we can take is to set aside the personal ego's limited awareness and let Universal Mind/Spirit/God guide us through the maze of experience.

The Ultimate Teacher

A student may attend the most prestigious universities filled with professors with impressive credentials and academic achievements—and from a worldly understanding, one would tend to believe that these are the ultimate sources of teaching and knowledge. In such worshipping of traditional academia, the concept of a teaching from a higher source becomes blurred. Scholastic achievement, whether secular or non-secular, becomes the idealized goal.

Yes, to suggest that life's ultimate teacher is God seems naïve when compared to what can be learned in traditional academia, or even in a faith-based traditional university that acknowledges God's Presence as the ultimate teacher. Faith-based university institutions can still fail, as students become but parrots, echoing the dogma of the particular theology of that denomination. Life is then scripted from outside sources rather than created by the guidance of the Inner Source or God, the ultimate teacher.

One of the greatest examples of learning from the ultimate teacher was Jesus, himself. While learning extensively from what Judaism offered in his day, it was still too limited. It spoke about God and how God wanted one to live, but not how to be taught by God directly. What it produced parallels traditional religious universities of today—the parroting of theologies, rather than teaching directly from God's Presence within oneself. This does not create whole people, which should be the goal of learning—but rather birds of a feather (that is, collective parroting).

Now those who have mystical awareness are not upset by the scholastics of this world, knowing that the vast majority of souls that incarnate into the physical plane of Earth's existence are not ready for ultimate teaching and so must be taught by the standards of lesser awareness. Most assuredly, traditional academia is valuable in producing technicians and experts trained in traditional specialties to help others, such as medical teachings and the various sciences and arts. But it is not ultimately valuable, except for those very, very few, whole and complete people who are, in addition, taught by the ultimate teacher or God.

Candidly, if a person has awakened to mystical awareness, such as the inner mystical union with God's Presence within themselves, only then are they taught by the ultimate teacher—Universal Consciousness, Spirit, or God. It is only then that the knowledge of academia is seen in an entirely new way. And that is because the person has also become whole and complete, where wisdom and the living of it from the ultimate teacher teach a way of life.

True wisdom, synonymous with true spirituality, cannot be taught by outside scholastic sources, but is received as a gift from God when a soul is ready for an awakening to greater realities beyond the sensory impressions of the physical world.

War and Peace—
A Mystical Perspective

Souls who wish peace on Earth to enjoy what peace has to offer to themselves and to those they love, dream of peace on this planetary dimension. In the history of this Earth plane, there have been times of peace depending on one's geographical location; and, thus, a person might idealize that permanent, lasting peace is possible.

Were it only so!

With mystical awareness comes the knowing that on this Earth plane, it will never be so. This is a plane of existence whose very existence is based on dualism or opposites. Hot and cold, pleasure or pain, love or loneliness, and, should it not then follow, war and peace.

This is a plane of existence that is a landing place for souls who are caught up in conflicts within themselves and thus incarnate into an environment that is in harmony with the turmoil within themselves. Not being to a point in spiritual awakening where they can deal with the inner demons that plague their souls, they are easy recruits to project inner conflicts into environmental conflicts or wars.

Of course there are souls who wish only peace to prevail; but, because of the peace that is part of their natures, they fail to stop the world's war tyrants until they have acquired sufficient force, momentum, and followers to do harm to non-aggressive souls.

As night follows day, on this Earth plane, war follows peace. This does not only occur in the Earth plane, but other dimensions of existence, as well. Wherever there is duality, souls who are in conflict will incarnate where dualism or conflict is inevitable.

It all started when souls fell from oneness and became personal ego identities—not only disassociated from God, but also from each other. It was the breeding ground for dualistic manifestations, opposites, opposite sides—wars.

No soul can find lasting peace on this Earth plane of existence, which thus magnifies the mystics' credo—that the only way out, is in. Peace that is lasting can be only found in Eternal peace that is oneness or God within oneself. What can one do in this world of inevitable conflicts?

Teach, teach, teach—for a few souls are ready to know and act—that the way out—is in. This dissolves the cycle of birth and rebirth onto this Earth plane of existence or other similar planes and elevates one even beyond the planes where Gods and Goddesses exist— for, yes—even they have their conflicts.

Yes, there is that existence of the highest souls, where souls are so close to God, that it could be said that every breath they breathe is God's breath, where all is eternal oneness, love—peace.

In gratitude to the eternal peace that is God within you!

Time ???
A Mystical Perspective

A person remembers the past and wonders about the future. An older person thinks how quickly time has passed—that it seemed just yesterday—perhaps even a moment ago, that they were as young as the youth they see around them.

Yes, as the expression goes, time "seems to fly by"—but does it?

On the other hand, people describing some great moment of inspiration have said or written that it was as if "time stood still."

On this physical Earth plane and dimension of existence, in order to have existence as a person perceives it with his or her outer senses—it is a world of opposites, and that includes what seems to appear as past and present.

With mystical awareness, there is the reality that past and present on this Earth plane are opposites, but when one is in Universal Consciousness, God, oneness, or absolute reality, there are no opposites. There is simply the eternal moment of beingness, a singular moment of God's eternal contemplation—"I am."

When the Christ Mind that was in Jesus spoke the words, "I am Alpha and Omega, the beginning and the end," it expressed a great truth of beingness—that the beginning and end are one.

Stepping back and pausing in one's mind long enough to escape the illusion of opposites brings the realization that if the beginning and ending are one— then there is no room for anything in between or past or future—or time, as it is humanly perceived.

Hinduism expresses the world of Earth plane existence as *Maya*—the great illusion. If time exists in this illusion, then time itself is an illusion.

With the advancement of technology, will the fascinating concept of time travel come to pass—or at least seem to? What would this really mean?

One could visit either the past (?) or speed ahead to the future (?) could visit today's Earth or the past (?). A person from the future (?) could visit today's Earth or the past (?). A person from today's Earth could visit the past (?) or the future (?). With mystical awareness there is the knowingness that the past (?) and the future (?) exist simultaneously as one eternal moment, and that in reality, all stand still in the "peace that passeth all understanding"—that is, Universal Consciousness or God.

To discern the truth of life despite the illusion is to become more and more aware of the Universal

Consciousness or God within oneself, inspired by the only reality that is—God's eternal presence in the eternal moment of now.

Incarnation by Choice, or by Energy Filtering

Nothing in this Universe is by chance. All that is taking place throughout the vastness of Universal Presence is interconnected in the most precise way to every soul on the physical Earth plane. The life that everyone is leading is intertwined with this vast universal process, consciousness that is God.

Incarnating of souls into various planes, dimensions, or physically perceived planets is part of the universal process, for the smallest particles of existence are as important to the functioning of universal life as is the whole of universal life itself.

Again, nothing is by chance. The dimension/planet that a soul incarnates on, the parent souls that the soul physically incarnates through—all are by divine design. All souls incarnate precisely where they are supposed to—through the vehicles of the physical parent souls that they are supposed to—whether seemingly to the advantage or disadvantage of the incarnating soul.

The process for the vast majority of incarnating souls is automatic; that is, they do not have a say in the choice of parents or environment they incarnate through and into. All is based on the energy frequencies of what stage of awareness to the whole or God and the will of the Universe that a soul is in.

The universal process, like a giant filtering machine, automatically directs the path into a new incarnation. Again, this involves the majority of souls incarnating into this physical, Earth plane dimension. They have not awakened sufficiently to the whole or God consciousness to make the choice for themselves—and thus, the choice is made for them through the universal energy frequency filtering process.

Angry, hostile energy souls will incarnate where there is a greater likelihood of wars and conflicts. Peaceful souls will incarnate into areas where there is a more peaceful environment. This could be thought of as karma on a larger collective stage of incarnating souls. Collective or group incarnations are also part of the automatic filtering process that, in the language of this physical Earth plane, is described as generational.

The only exceptions to the automatic filtering process are universally awakened souls who are totally aware of the life that they are incarnating into and are able before incarnation to see and know how their lives will be lived. They have the awakening sufficient enough to make the choice whether to incarnate or not.

Yet—this is not a personal choice. Because they are universally aware, they are part of universal or God's Will, and thus it is universal or God's Will that truly makes the choice. These souls—totally in tune with the Spirit—choose the will of the whole that they are part of.

Incarnating, for a universally awakened soul, is for the purpose of helping souls who are not yet awakened, to assist in that awakening, knowing that only a few are ready for total awakening and that at least the seeds for the blossoming of awakening can be planted in the soil of the mind to come into fruition in some future incarnation.

So it's been through eternity—to awaken the few—and make ready the majority.

It can be described as incarnating in the grander scheme of things.

May your part be lived to its fullest!

Who's Really Who?
Angels, Gods, Higher Beings—
a Mystical Perspective

Most who have traveled the path of metaphysical, and more specifically, mystical spirituality, agree that there is but one ultimate life, Universal Consciousness, Spirit, or God throughout the Universe, existing on and as multiple dimensions of expression. Between human consciousness as it currently exists in the majority of people and the ultimate supreme consciousness, or God, there exists a wide divide that eventually every soul must experience when awakening to the ultimate reality or God.

Throughout recorded history, people have described visions of higher beings. They have been described as angelic, god- or goddess-like, or Christ-like, Buddha-like, Krishna-like, and so on. When such experiences occur, the recipient feels inspired. Nothing needs be spoken in the traditional way of human communication; instead, there is an exchange of energy as the communication. The person who has had such a vision or visions feels a greater certainty that there are higher beings that exist in higher dimensions of consciousness, giving rise to an assurance that there is life beyond this physical dimension and that life can exist in a higher, more spiritual way than earthly existence.

Indeed, life of a higher order can and does exist in higher dimensions of universal consciousness. Yet, there is far more to such realizations than people having such visions are aware of, until they are more awakened to what they are really seeing.

Most people having visions of higher beings will see them as some higher order of life, something to be looked up to. This is the response of the personal ego and its limited awareness. Just as more primitive forms of religion cause a great divide between humans and God, so, too, this same divide that is part of personal ego consciousness perceives such visions of higher beings to be separate or apart from themselves—something to be idolized, but nothing to specifically identify with their own existences.

Stop for a moment—lean back in the armchair of your mind and ponder: there is but one ultimate life, Universal Consciousness, or God. Everyone is an individualized expression or manifestation of the one life. Ultimately, there are no two of anything, but one that is everything.

Everyone is inseparable from God's One Life Presence, and all is of the one life presence, whether on the human life earthly physical plane or what is perceived as higher beings on higher dimensions of existence.

Who's Who?

When people experience higher beings, they are not experiencing beings apart from themselves. In truth, they are experiencing higher dimensions of themselves, or, more specifically, what they will be through ongoing spiritual awakening.

All that ever will be—already is. That includes what every soul will ever be. Everything—past, present and future—exists in one eternal moment of time.

When people have visions of higher beings—angels, gods, goddesses, or higher—they are seeing how they themselves will manifest in the future, or the dominate expression of being that they will be living; they are seeing themselves as they will be—and in reality— already are. They are seeing what is before them that fills the divide in consciousness between limited human ego awareness and oneness with the ultimate Universal, God Consciousness, Spirit—God.

Life is one. Oneness is love, and everyone is one with all that is—and the higher beauty and awareness that they already are.

Today's visions—tomorrow's realities.

Healing—A Mystical Perspective

There are many who present themselves as healers, as well as many methods of treatment—f rom the most primitive to even what is described as the science of today. Everything has its place and time in the Universe—the Universe in mystical reality being the thought process of Universal Consciousness or God. And, if everything indeed does have its place and time in human experience, inclusive of healing, then in the human expression or practice of healing there is no "one size fits all" manner of treatment or one kind of healer above all others.

From a mystical perspective, healing and healers are viewed from what in fact is really taking place. Consider, by way of example, Jesus, who had seemingly—at least in appearance's sake—performed miracles of healing. When credit was directed toward him, he responded, through the Christ Mind that was in him, with the words: "Why callest me good? It is not I, but the Father which doeth these good works." He spoke the great mystical truth about healing, healers, and healing methods—only the Universal Consciousness or God actually does the healing.

The claim that any one healer or healing method does the actual healing is a ploy of the personal ego trying to substantiate or give credence to the thought that it even exists. Contrasts, contradictions of wellness, or sickness, healing methods, and healers are all part of the foundational fabric that creates the illusion that there are many lives, a great variety, rather than the one singular life of God. Yes, healing can be part of Maya or illusion that anything can take place independently of the whole—or God. Yet, if a person who has been ill experiences a healing, it is not because of any specific healing method or healer. It is, by the simplest of all terms familiar to most—"By the grace of God."

To mystically understand healing, healers, and methodologies, we must come from the mystical awareness that life is a universal process, and all that is taking place is part of the functioning of universal process. To maintain the Universe/Universes, physical dimension/other dimensions, all must coordinate to serve the whole—universal will or God's Will. Health, lack of it, healing, healers, and methods are part of the ongoing universal process which is life—and they sustain life as it appears to the physical senses.

Mystically awakened healers—and there are but a few—realize that they are a part of the illusion of life through the physical senses; they have their roles to play in the universal process. The methods or treatments they use are to fill a time gap between the appearance of sickness and wellness. They realize that if a healing takes place from a physical sense perspective, it is because it is the appropriate time and place in the universal process; the healing is something that has already taken place in the one eternal moment that is God's Presence.

As Albert Schweitzer once said, "It is the role of the physician to amuse the patient long enough, to give nature (God) the time to actually do the healing." What then of those not healed? In actuality the healing already is at a higher level of Universal Consciousness or God-Mind. It is a matter of the illusion's catching up to reality, or the personal ego's awakening more fully to God's Presence. Perhaps that illness or lack of wellness even causes the human being to have the time to evaluate his or her life and self-adjust to the soul's purpose as part of the ongoing universal process that is life—or God.

In the light, to serve the light that is God—be well!

To Know Everything, Admit to Knowing Nothing

There is nothing so ignorant as the personal ego, that believes it knows something, or anything, about the reality of life.

The personal ego is itself a figment of the mind's illusion and imagination that has been created from one's limited physical sense perceptions. Individuals have come to believe that it exists and has actual reality. How can anything that is of itself a non-reality even begin to attempt to grasp the actual reality of what life really is, both on a universal scale and miniaturized down to an individual?

The personal ego binds and restricts an understanding of life as a whole and an individual's relationship to life. Oftentimes, one person, sensing that another person is being deluded about something, will exclaim, "Get real!" But how can individuals really get real, if what they have to work with—their personal egos—are unreal in and of themselves?

This truth is brought up in the following Biblical verse: "He who loses himself (that is, the personal ego) for my sake (that is, Universal Consciousness or God) finds himself (that is, that truth about God within—self, reality, Christ Self, Mind, or Consciousness of Christ)."

When a person has finally discarded the illusionary sense of the personal ego's unreality, the consciousness is free to experience Universal Christ, Buddha, or Krishna awareness of the reality of Life—the true relationship of individual human creation and existence to the greater totality of the Will of God. Till such time, the mind or consciousness within the individual wanders amongst shadowy images within itself, believing that the images are reality and remaining unaware that to have shadows, there must be light—the light that to the mystic is the light of creation—or God.

If truth be ultimately known—the world, or physical-plane earthly life, is but a mixture of shadows. Science, as it currently exists, is an attempt to classify and understand shadows rather than to search more directly into the light source—or life Itself. Very few of today's scientists are exceptions to this. Only those few are God-motivated from within themselves to discover the ultimate first cause.

To awaken to universal consciousness where ultimate reality and one's relationship to it can be known, necessitates the admission by one's very soul that the imaginary "I" or personal self in truth knows nothing in regard to life and is speculating only on the meaning of shadows.

Only when a soul truly knows its reason for existing can the fulfilment of the soul be achieved, which, in truth, is God's Will individualized. To know everything is to know one's relationship to everything, the universal eternal beingness of God. To know one's relationship to God is to know one's soul's purpose, or the reason for your being an individualized expression of God's Presence.

Without such awareness—be it likened to Christ, Buddha, or Krishna—the mind remains a dimly lit room with choices and decisions about life based on shadowy speculations. When life is so founded, it is no wonder there is so much failure in the human experience to live in happiness and fulfillment.

It is not enough to acknowledge intellectually what is written here. That's only a philosophical agreement, which still falls under the province of the personal ego. To know everything—God—you must admit to knowing nothing. The Christ Mind that was in Jesus alluded to this in the words, "Unless you become as little children (that is, stripped of the personal ego's intellect), you shall not enter the Kingdom of Heaven (that is, the Beingness of God Consciousness)."

The choice is to remain a shadowy figure or to step into the light of one's light-self. When you are ready, the light will guide you unto itself.

Love in Extremes: Lacking It or Being It

Who can deny that loving is life's greatest experience, except those persons who, from lack of it, turn to substitutes such as an obsession for power over others through force, intimidation, manipulation, and fear? Yes, the tyrant, the terrorist, and the followers are so empty of love in their consciousness that they go to extremes to fill the vacuum within their minds. Those who commit the greatest atrocities are those who lack the vibration, the energy, and the presence of love in their lives.

Moreover, those who lack love's presence in their lives are those who lack God's Presence in their lives, making them easy prey for the leader who uses the name of God to give credibility to his rallying cry. The recruits are plentiful, for the underworld—those more hellish, lower astral planes—houses souls ready to incarnate and lash out from the lack of love of God in their lives.

These souls harbor an anguish that feels, "if I hurt so much, I will hurt others." And, mystically viewed, the lack of love or God's Presence is the greatest of all hurts. Those who suffer the most from it are those who are most unaware of the actual cause of why they are hurting or why they wish to lash out at others under the veneer of a cause that God supposedly favors.

God being love can never, of course, condone anything that is anti-love. For a leader to suggest heavenly rewards for living and expressing the opposite of love or God—through commission of atrocities—only demonstrates the total antithesis to love or God's Presence and the great void of love or God that exists in such levels of consciousness.

To speak of the value of love is to know something of the Presence of God. Only in oneness is love or God possible in one's life. Mystically, there is but One Life in this Universe: everything that exists, seen and unseen, in the physical dimension or other dimensions, in this universe or multi-universes, is the same one presence. Love is the experience of oneness, whether for an individual within one's family or the family of humankind. The Biblical quotation "Love thy neighbor as thyself" could be mystically expanded to, "Love thy neighbor as thyself, for thy neighbor is thyself."

Mystically—every time you feel love—you are feeling God's Presence. When someone feels love, whether it be in a personal love relationship, toward a family member, toward a friend, or in an expanded version to the entirety of humanity, that person is experiencing God's Presence. When mystics through the ages have tried to express what they experienced as being God's Presence, they could only describe it as oneness with all and, in that absolute oneness—absolute love.

It is very apparent then that the personal ego, which produces a consciousness of division, is the inner barrier to love or God: the less personal ego—the more presence of love or God. When the personal ego has been replaced with God's Love or Presence, then a person is the embodiment of love or living God's Presence. One's life then is the expression of love, or God—not confined to only a small select circle—but for the greater good of all humanity.

When this is achieved, one has even bypassed wisdom and its delights and instead lives beyond words or thoughts, for words or thoughts pale in their value and are not even necessary when there is the presence of love—or God.

To the degree that one lives without ego is the measure of living God's Love Presence.

Universal God Beingness: An Expanded Mystical View

Simply put, when you look out at the physical Universe, you look into one level of universal mind consciousness or the Mind of God. And, through the physical instruments of today's science, the further out into the farthest reaches of the Universe you look—the deeper into your own consciousness you can enter.

The Biblical words, "as above, so below," can be taken quite literally. It is a mystical reality that speaks the eternal truth that all life is one and the same, and that ultimately there is but one life everywhere present—be it in the vastness of what appears as outer space or in the more finite existence of a human, from the appearance of the tremendous mass of a star to the appearance of a pebble or a droplet of water—each comes from one universal life consciousness manifesting as us all.

Referencing again the Bible, the words "within Him, we move, live, and have our being" have a profound literal meaning when understood mystically. Quite literally, all that exists, moves, lives, and has its beingness comes from within the Mind of God, just as all that is visible—both in the seen physical world and the unseen dimensional worlds—exists in the Mind of God or Universal Consciousness.

All forms of existence are thought form images existing in the Universal Consciousness or the Mind of God. The physical dimension is but one level in the Mind of God or Universal Consciousness. Just as there are structures of human consciousness (such as the conscious level, the personal subconscious level, the astral level), in similar fashion there exists the multiple levels of the Mind of God or Universal Consciousness.

The often-spoken words "man is made in the image and likeness of God" are mystical clarification to this reality. The words image and likeness of God are not referring to the appearance of human form and shape, but rather to consciousness as the miniaturization of Universal Consciousness and its working structures or levels manifesting as human consciousness. As above, so below: the microcosm is a reflection of the macrocosm.

Just as a person is self-aware, so too the Universe is self-aware, but as an all-inclusive universal self. The Universe is existent on so many levels of self-awareness: planets as they travel in their orbits, thoughts circling around a central theme, or any physical existence in the physically perceived universe. All are thought processes within the Mind of God or Universal Consciousness. Just as in the human mind, where central themes of thought are born and then pass away—so too stars, or what might be described as star themes, come into existence and then pass away in the thought process of Universal Consciousness or the Mind of God.

The Psalmist uttered the words, "you are fearfully and wonderfully made," a reality that can only be grasped by those who have taken the mystical voyage into their own consciousness.

What has all of this to do with the human life of anyone? Can such awareness of reality serve any practical purpose in the life of a human being?

Resoundingly—yes!

Life is a matter of awareness. The more aware we are, the more we are aware of what is taking place in our lives and, more importantly, our role—or soul's purpose—within it. Meditation awakens one's consciousness, and conscious awareness creates greater sensitivity to what is—and what is not—both on a Universal scale and the individual's role within it.

As individuals go through their days, it is to their practical advantage to—at least for a few moments daily—be aware of both who they are—a thought form purpose according to the Will of God—and where they are—in the thought process of Universal Life Consciousness or the Mind of God. In such a state of awareness and recognition, access to God's Guidance is not then a thing one seeks, but rather what one is a part of.

Therefore, live in awareness of greater reality, that life may reflect such awareness to the glory and acknowledgement of God's Mind, in whom all have been created.

Programmed Longevity or Universal Timekeeping

There is, as the expression goes, "a time for all seasons." This very fundamental truth of universal experience applies to every soul entering or exiting this physical Earth dimension. Nothing in this Universe is by chance. Everything and everyone is part of a very integrated and complex universal process. Entire species have appeared and disappeared from the Earth plane dimension. Everything has its time, or at least, the appearance of it. Everything exists and comes into being in Universal Consciousness or the Mind of God.

There is a larger picture—the Universe—with smaller details in the picture, such as the individual human expression. And yet the larger and the smaller are identical, and everything therefore is interdependent—that is, one could not exist without the other. As the seen universe is always in motion, all of its parts or details or humans are part of a very integrated process. What happens with one of its parts—the human—affects the entire whole and how it manifests. Each depends on the existence of the other in order to exist itself.

A total picture, to be a total picture, is dependent on the sum of its details, while concurrently the details could not exist if they were not a part of the total picture. What is taking place in one human life, even if that one human were totally isolated and lived on a far-off mountain or cave, affects and interacts with all that exists—with millions in a bustling cosmopolitan city on the physical Earth plane as well as the cosmos.

Because of this unfathomable interaction between a Universal Whole constantly in process and the sum of its parts or humans, nothing is left to chance. All must be coordinated or there would be monumental chaos on a Universal scale. If one subscribes to the Big Bang theory—imagine an endless series of Big Bangs with chaotic presence through eternity.

All of this comes back to a season and time for all things—a season to be born and a time to die, a season to have one's soul move from inhabiting a human body on to its next expression or manifestation. Think of the Universal Presence as one large cosmic clock. Everything that exists is part of the mechanism, or in this case, the integrated and interacting parts of universal timing. This means that everything that is born will be born, have its season or timed existence in a certain dimensional time, and then move on to a different dimensional time.

All human beings have a certain amount of preprogrammed time to exist in this physical Earth dimension. This is part of their spiritual DNA, as it were. Whether to live only a few seconds after physical birth or to live on to be a centenarian—all is a matter of being coordinated with the Universal Consciousness or the Will of God. If a person survives a horrific accident or a critical surgery or any other physically life-threatening experience, it was because he or she was programmed so according to universal timing or the Will of God.

In universal reality, one cannot escape fate—for what will be, already is. What supposedly will happen has already happened, for we exist in the eternal moment of time. Everyone has a certain amount of time or existence within the outer appearance of the passing of time—in time's illusion—not one moment less or one moment more. Everyone's existence is reliant on the creation and continuation by Universal Consciousness or God.

In mystical reality, God is the real and only life of one's soul and human embodiment. And thus, trust that God knows best the timing of every human's life expression or the longevity of Spirit in expression.

What to do?

- Live one's life to the fullest, with the good of all and the Will of God in mind, as if each day were the last.
- Do the very best one can. It does not matter that one is the very best—only that one does one's best.

Be at peace, for God controls longevity.

After Enlightenment—
Then What?

There are at this very moment many people throughout the world following many different spiritual paths they hope will bring them to what they believe is the very end of the spiritual rainbow—enlightenment.

People traveling the various paths to enlightenment feel that if they can achieve it, then they have achieved the Ultimate human experience. Enlightenment, in its truest description, goes beyond intellectual comprehension of the experience. It is not about seeking God, speculating, or theologically theorizing about God or ultimate beingness. Enlightenment means the firsthand, intimate, mystical experience of God Presence or oneness with the Universe. It is beingness with ultimate beingness itself—in consciousness at its innermost center yet also to its outer reaches universally.

If all that is being stated is accurate, it would indeed seem that experiencing Enlightenment would be the end of a journey through countless lifetimes for the soul, the individualized expression of ultimate beingness, consciousness, Spirit or God. What else is there? If, in the next moment, one would suddenly experience Enlightenment, would life come to an abrupt halt? Would one's soul be swallowed up by an infinite field of light, with one's physical body vanishing as a result?

The history of enlightened people reads otherwise. Physical life continues on the outside, and, to family, friends, and work associates, such persons outwardly look much the same: They don't have visible auras around their heads. Outwardly, life seems to go on as it was—at least in the time right after the experience. They may speak of it to a few they feel would not think them mentally unbalanced. But, for the most part, they remain silent, knowing that few would believe, and, as such, it would be better left unsaid. The exception would be those very few souls whose life purpose would be to teach that such an experience of a higher ultimate reality is possible.

So, what happens after enlightenment for the others? In short, they become living energy expressions of the experience. What this means is that their lives are under the influence of a Will higher than their personal wills—that consciously or unconsciously, each will feel that, as the Mind of Christ that was in Jesus expressed it, "I am about my Father's business." In this state of beingness, Enlightened persons go about their days bringing or expressing greater love and creativity in whatever they are involved. Everything is done under universal influence, and even when one stumbles or appears to fail, one is being guided to a higher plateau of consciousness.

Each will do things better in life because of being so guided, although, again, this may not be evident in the worldly definition of success. Fame, fortune, notoriety, and worldly power are not sought after, for, with enlightenment such goals are seen as what they are: grand illusions of the personal ego and its constricted view of what life is.

Again, after enlightenment, a person's life outwardly may seem little different to others: Family life will go on, sexuality will go on, sickness and health will go on, failure and success will go on. But inwardly, the personal ego is no longer in charge, for the person is marching to a different drummer, the drumbeat being orchestrated by the ultimate Universal Life Presence—or God to guide the soul's path and this life.

Yes—there is life after enlightenment. A very wonderful life; for, each will, in a short time after the experience or at some point in the person's lifetime, become fully conscious and aware that his or her life is being fully guided by ultimate beingness or God. The awareness of this intimacy of consciousness with the Supreme is the great gift to one's mind, peace to one's soul, and love's ultimate presence for one's spiritual heart of hearts.

The Illusion of Co-Creating and the Reality of Aligned Co-Creating

From traditional and fundamentalist dogma to metaphysical speculations, the basic belief has been that the power of God can intervene in human affairs to somehow provide people what they believe they need. A very large percentage of any organized or even non-organized religion has had such belief as the foundation of its existence. In the most basic of terms, most human beings are attracted to some form of religion based on what they believe the religion can do for them in their present physical lives and as some assurance of good experience in any afterlife. In effect, the religion (at least in a follower's mind) acts as an intermediary between the follower and God. Reduced to its simplest description, people become part of a religion with the thought that through the religion of their choice, God will grant them their desires or prayers in this life and the afterlife.

When humans are very young, they look up to their physical parents to supply their needs. When they become adults, at least in number of physical years, they turn to God to take over for their physical parents to supply their needs during their physical lifetime and in the life beyond the physical. In traditional religion, God is prayed to—asked, pleaded with, or begged—that something be granted.

In more metaphysical spirituality, nothing is asked, but affirmed that in the mind of God, it is already theirs. In some of the more unaware attempts at metaphysical spirituality, people are taught that God or Universal Mind is like a magic genie that will do for them whatever the individual egos wish or command it to do. Then there is still another concept, which suggests that a person join with God to co-create whatever the individual ego is seeking.

Now, there is the reality that has not yet been mentioned—the mystical reality that is aware that personal ego does not know what is best for the soul. Only God or Universal Consciousness knows, and living life with the concept that the personal ego can petition Universal Mind or God to join in a process of co-creating is an illusion. God Mind or Universal Mind will not enter into a co-creative process to provide anything just because the will of the personal ego so desires. Only when the Will of God or the Universe is served will any form of a co-creative process with a human being ever be entered into.

This reality is that God Mind places into human conscious awareness what it should do, want, or desire. In essence, human consciousness can agree to co-create with the Will of God, to align itself with the Universal Will such that the Will of God or Spirit be done through the soul and its outward, physical form expression. Thus, what can be called aligned co-creating refers to the soul in human form expression in alignment with Universal Will. In this way, the soul and its human form expression are working in harmony with universal life process ad infinitum.

So—what to do?

Mystics who have achieved true enlightenment or union with God are fully aware that they live to do the Will of God. The needs of the personal ego are set aside, while the Will of God Consciousness and the role of the soul in God Consciousness take priority. The words from the Bible echo this truth—"not my will (personal ego), but Thy will be done."

Until one has experienced enlightenment or mystical oneness with God, every day maintain an awareness that, "Thy Will, not mine be done." When you pray, ask that God's Will for your soul be made known to your conscious awareness. Pray for divine God guidance for your mind to be aligned with the Will of God for your soul. Every day seek to diminish the illusion of a personal ego identity and its will.

After enlightenment, one should do the very same, for it will still take time for universal identity to be fully in charge while the personal ego struggles to retain its illusionary control.

And for those seeking an upgraded afterlife experience, the words from the Christ Mind that was in Jesus provide counsel—"Unless a man doeth the Will of the Father, he cannot enter the Kingdom of Heaven."

The kingdom of heaven is both a higher, heavenly aware consciousness while still in physical life embodiment as well as an afterlife heavenly environment.

Be in aligned co-creating with Universal God Mind/Spirit and be one with the words, "on Earth as it is in heaven."

Decision Making: Who Makes the Decisions?

How life turns out, or how it is going for anyone is based on what decisions one has made, to one's betterment or detriment.

When a soul is born into this physical earthly dimension, he or she incarnates, with but few exceptions, with a false sense of identity—the personal ego. The limited sense of awareness surrounded by other personal egos as they grow to adulthood reinforces the illusion that they are but personal ego identities.

From schoolyard adolescence to the adult environments of human life in this earthly dimension, the personal ego identity is accepted as being the decision maker in one's life. The personal ego becomes involved in a personal learning process from what one's parents believe and then expands into the beliefs of educators, politicians, scientists, and, for the majority, religions. The personal ego builds what it knows about life and how to live it based on a composite from all these sources of what is and what is not.

From the composite of sources emerges what the personal ego will base its decision making on. This will not only affect the life of any one soul, but just as importantly, the lives of others who interact with this soul as it moves through its earthly lifetime—and yes, beyond this incarnation into an afterlife. Whatever affects one speck of life or a human being, affects the whole or the Universe, as the speck is an active part of the whole.

The false sense of the personal ego identity recognizes, to a limited extent, that what it does affects others, but because of the very limitation of the personal ego, it does not grasp to what extent. Viewed in this context, what one does in one's life has a ripple effect throughout life on a universal scale. What people choose to do as life's choices unfold before them is thus based on their decision making.

"To be, or not to be" could be seen as a very wise question: "To be [a universal reality identity], or not to be [to remain a limited, false, personal ego identity]." Indeed, that is the question. To the point: will one's decision making be made as a result of the opinions of others accumulated in the memory consciousness of the personal ego, or will one's decisions be inspired intuitively by the only real identity—universal God Presence? Will the decisions arrived at be powered by the will of the false personal ego, or the one true life of God's Universal Presence manifesting its Spirit through the soul and the surface mind awareness of a person?

It is a choice between living by one's wits (or personal ego), as the saying goes, or by the wisdom of the ages past, present, and future that flows inspirationally and intuitively through oneself. To the mystic who has pierced through the veil of outer sense perception and has glimpsed the greater reality that is real life and real identity, it is not a matter of choosing false, personal ego identity or real universal identity, for there can only be universal God Presence and Will as the source of all decision making in one's life.

If a person has not yet awakened to mystical awareness and alignment with the Universal God Will in decision making but at least intellectually or philosophically recognizes the wisdom to have Wisdom be the decision maker in one's life, then the best advice is to be certain to make meditation practice a part of everyday—and continually remind one's self that the personal ego is a myth of outer sensory illusions. If this is done with purity of heart and the selflessness of the Spirit vibrating in one's soul, decision making will be made by universal God Presence.

Please take serious note that a person whose decision making is being guided by universal God Presence will not always have what would appear to be a positive outcome by worldly standards. Recognize this as a temporary adjustment by Spirit to one's soul journey; for, when all the cosmic dust has settled and one looks back in hindsight, the blessing of such an outcome will be apparent.

So, under God Presence, even when decision making may not seem to be working things out for the physical moment, know that they really are being worked out in the eternal moment—and after all, that's where one really lives and has eternal beingness.

Realities and Absurdities of Religion

The one reality all religions share is that there is a God—a supreme being. Beyond that one commonly shared view—it's downhill into absurdities.

The main absurdity, about which most people are familiar, is the clerical manipulation that "ours is the only religion." As this is an Earth plane dimension that for the most part attracts souls with limited spiritual awareness, promoting this concept is easy for souls looking and needing spiritual assurance and desperate for hope. Under this banner "ours is the only religion," prejudices have been formed, wars have been fought—all not to perpetuate the Will of God, but rather for the power of clerical manipulators.

The reality is that there are many different levels of spiritual awareness by souls who have through history incarnated onto this planet. As such, the Super-consciousness that a person would attribute to God would of course know that souls would need something they can relate to at a level that they can respond to. This is why God has allowed so many different religions to exist and even so many factions within different religions. Of course, the clerical manipulators do not want to hear such reality and wish to drown it out under their zealous shouts that "ours is the only religion." In reality, any religion whose clerical manipulators claim that theirs is the only religion and that this is cause for all other religions to be eliminated is not Godly, but against God's Will that has provided many religions or ways to have God present in one's life.

It can be justly pointed out here that the International Metaphysical Ministry recognizes the reality that God has made many religions so that all souls at every level might have a way that God can be in their lives. If anyone who has ever been ordained by the IMM begins to proclaim that his or her religion is the only way to find, know, or associate with God, that person would no longer be recognized by the IMM; such an unfortunate soul has gone off the deep ego-end into the abyss of religion's elitism and absurdity.

God-guided countries? "Yes." One-religion guided countries? Emphatically, "No."

Another absurdity promoted by the male gender of clerical manipulators is that souls incarnating in female bodies are somehow second-class souls and should be subservient to souls incarnating in male bodies.

The reality is that God did not create the female gender to serve the male gender—nor conversely males to serve women. The reality is that Spirit has provided the dualistic illusion of male and female in physical form so that each should serve God's Presence in each other. Find a religion that places women in a secondary role to the men in its hierarchy, and one disrobes a Godless religion, regardless of its high sounding platitudes. Male and female energies are created equally by God to give dualistic illusion for the life beyond the one life of God and for the sake of balance—necessary to avoid chaos in manifestation beyond the primal spirit. Only a religion, or a society for that matter, that recognizes the equality of both the masculine and feminine can make any realistic claim to being guided by God or a manifestation in earthly or other-dimensional form connected to the ultimate life presence or God.

A much longer exploration of the realities and absurdities found in religions could certainly be continued. What has been pointed to are the two major absurdities to be found in religions, together with the realities that totally negate their assertions. If religions will begin to recognize the God-willed necessity for the existence of each other—that every soul may have a way to relate to God according to its level of spiritual awareness—then can God's peace both figuratively and literally be manifested by religion on Earth.

Perhaps the golden rule could be applied to religions—do unto other religions as you would have other religions do unto you.

Bottom spiritual line—God has created both of you.

About the Author

As far back as he could remember, Paul Leon Masters was drawn to the mysteries of life, the universe, the mind, the soul, and the Presence of a Higher Intelligence—or God—behind creation. In his teens, he decided to pursue his interests by becoming a member of the Rosicrucians and the Mayans (similar to the Rosicrucians, but based in Texas).

A Thirst for the Mystical

What he studied caused him to thirst for more knowledge about the mystical as well as any form of psychology that had an appreciation of the mystical. He also found that what he had learned, when applied to the lives of others, seemed to help them. This led him to seek a school that had a degree program in tune with the mystical/psychological path he wished to pursue. Traditional universities, particularly in the 1950s, did not offer anything close to what he was seeking.

The Institute of Parapsychology

He kept searching until finding a nontraditional school where he could learn more about mystical teachings, as well as spiritual psychology. In 1953 he enrolled in that college, a metaphysically-oriented religious school. He graduated with a doctorate in 1959 and went on to found his own metaphysical research and teaching organization: the Institute of Parapsychology, located in Beverly Hills. Still desirous of more knowledge, he enrolled in a second metaphysical college in 1960, this time focusing on New Thought teachings. He graduated with a second doctorate three years later.

Higher Consciousness Research

A true pioneer, in subsequent decades Dr. Masters spent countless hours with thousands of people conducting higher consciousness research—all of which enormously expanded what he originally learned in the 1950s and early 1960s. He founded the National Metaphysics Institute in 1965, conducting research on the spiritual heights and potentials of mind and spirit, which produced even more information from which he could teach.

Contributions to Mystical Psychology

His contributions to the field of mystical psychology were those of a trail-blazer. Having founded the University of Metaphysics (1976), he then founded the International Metaphysical Ministry (1989) to accommodate the world-wide interest and enrollment in his courses. Five years after that, he founded the University of Sedona (2003). He deservedly earned recognition as the world's foremost teacher of metaphysical doctors, teachers, and ministers, offering self-paced, distance learning degree programs in Holistic, New Thought, Theocentric, Transcendent, and Transpersonal Metaphysics. But the most important achievements of all Dr. Paul Masters' efforts were the support and advancement of higher consciousness research, education, and advanced New Thought Metaphysics.

Universal God Guidance from Within

As far as the wisdom and knowledge he gained, he gave full credit to prolonged contact with the Universal God Guidance from within himself during his experiences in higher consciousness meditation. People throughout the world, from all walks of life, have similarly heard an inner calling to help themselves help others through higher spiritual understanding and awareness. They have been able to fulfill their inner promptings as a result of learning about their true inner guidance as taught in the International Metaphysical Ministry's Universities of Sedona and Metaphysics.

Creating the World's Largest Non-Secular and Theological Schools

Both universities have a curriculum that is strictly non-secular and theological in nature, and they have become the world's largest schools of their kind, spanning 123 countries with over 10,000 students and graduates.

As he always wanted students and graduates to

have options to continue learning and keep current with new developments in the field, the universities now offer enrolled students and graduates an opportunity to participate in postgraduate Continuing Education. He recently added three new degrees in the University of Sedona for students to consider after they have completed the main doctoral program.

In addition, the websites and newsletters continue to offer tools and resources for self-development and uplifting humanity through the archives of inspirational weekly Video Lecture Broadcasts, Daily "Improve Your Life" Audio Messages, and the Mystical Insights teachings on Metaphysical Blog.

Reaching out to Transform the World

Supporting Dr. Masters' legacy in this endeavor is a highly qualified, dedicated professional administrative staff and knowledgeable Board of Directors, each having had many years of experience in the various aspects of the metaphysical field. Considering the dedication and experience of Dr. Masters and his staff, you will always be able to say with pride, "I received my doctoral degree from the most prominent, well respected metaphysical universities in the world—the University of Metaphysics and the University of Sedona."

From its beginning in 1959, the education he has provided has produced an international alumni and student population that continues learning and teaching the higher truth of human nature, reaching out to transform the world, one by one—to a world so very much in need of it.

www.metaphysics.com
www.universityofmetaphysics.com
www.universityofsedona.com
www.internationalmetaphysicalministry.com
www.voiceofmeditation.com

Index

207

Made in the USA
Middletown, DE
01 August 2017